The Complete Book of Bible Promises

Ron Rhodes

HARVEST HOUSE™ PUBLISHERS

Cover by Terry Dugan Design, Minneapolis, Minnesota

Published by Harvest House Publishers
Eugene, Oregon 97402

Library of Congress Cataloging-in-Publication Data
Rhodes, Ron.
The complete book of Bible promises / Ron Rhodes.
p. cm.
ISBN 0-7369-1206-1 (pbk.)
1. God—Promises—Biblical teaching. 2. Promise (Christian theology)—Biblical teaching. I. Title.
BS680.P68R48 2003
231.7—dc21 2003001885

Printed in the United States of America

03 04 05 06 07 08 09 10 / BP-MS / 10 9 8 7 6 5 4 3 2 1

To the glory of our faithful God,
who has "given us his very great
and precious promises"
(2 Peter 1:4).

Acknowledgments

Scripture proclaims that a good wife is "worth far more than rubies" (Proverbs 31:10), and that children are a gift from God (Psalm 127:3). What a fortunate man I am to have a wonderful wife, Kerri, and two wonderful children, David and Kylie. What did I ever do to deserve such blessing? As I write these words, I remember that this God of promises of whom Scripture speaks delights in giving us that which we do not deserve. Truly, God is ultimately deserving of praise and thanks for His wonderful blessing. May His name be exalted (Psalm 57:5,11)!

Contents

Peace like a River 7
The Blessedness of the Faith Life 9
Recognizing the Promises of God 13
When Life Throws You a Punch. 21
How to Use This Book 23

The Promises of God from A to Z 27

Appendix: God's Covenant Promises 275
Resources 279

Peace like a River

Every time I hear the story, my heart swells in praise to God for His faithfulness.

Horatio Gates Spafford was a personal friend of the great evangelist Dwight Moody. Spafford and his family decided to go on a vacation. The plan was to go to England in November 1873 to join Moody and Ira Sankey on an evangelistic crusade and then travel in Europe. Spafford had to attend to some last-minute business before he could leave, so he sent his family on ahead on a great ship—a French steamer called the *Ville de Havre.*

Tragically, the ship never reached its destination. It collided with another ship off the coast of Newfoundland and quickly sank. Only 47 of the 226 passengers survived. One of these was Spafford's wife, Anna. Their four young daughters—Maggie, Tanetta, Annie, and Bessie—drowned and perished in the harsh, icy waters. I can hardly imagine what Spafford must have felt when he received a telegram from his bereaved wife saying, "Saved alone."

Spafford immediately dropped all business and sailed to Europe to be with his wife. Upon reuniting, they met with Moody. Spafford said to him, "It is well. The will of God be done."

Some time after this overwhelming personal tragedy, Spafford penned the words to one of the most beloved hymns in Christian history, "It Is Well with My Soul." The lyrics stir the soul:

When peace like a river attendeth my way;
When sorrows like sea billows roll;
Whatever my lot, Thou hast taught me to say,
It is well, it is well with my soul.

(refrain)
It is well with my soul,
It is well, it is well with my soul.

Though Satan should buffet, though trials should come,
Let this blest assurance control,
That Christ hath regarded my helpless estate,
And hath shed His own blood for my soul.

(refrain)

My sin—oh, the bliss of this glorious thought—
My sin, not in part, but the whole,
Is nailed to the cross, and I bear it no more.
Praise the Lord, praise the Lord, O my soul.

(refrain)

And, Lord, haste the day when our faith shall be sight,
The clouds be rolled back as a scroll,
The trump shall resound, and the Lord shall descend;
Even so, it is well with my soul.

(refrain)

Surely Spafford's profound words were inspired by the wonderful promises of God. They enabled him, despite devastating grief, to rest in the peace and comfort that only God can give. God is faithful!

You may be facing deep waters and bitter trials in your own life. Dear friend, turn to God and trust in His promises. Supernatural tranquility and peace are available to you in every situation. They are yours for the taking. Cast yourself on God and His promises—and truly trust in Him—and this peace will be yours. He will sustain you. God is faithful!

Never forget that our God is a promise keeper. Numbers 23:19 asserts, "God is not a man, that he should lie, nor a son of man, that he should change his mind. Does he speak and then not act? Does he promise and not fulfill?" Prior to his death, an aged Joshua declared: "Now I am about to go the way of all the earth. You know with all your heart and soul that not one of all the good promises the LORD your God gave you has failed. Every promise has been fulfilled; not one has failed" (Joshua 23:14; see also Joshua 21:45). Solomon later proclaimed: "Praise be to the LORD, who has given rest to his people Israel just as he promised. Not one word has failed of all the good promises he gave through his servant Moses" (1 Kings 8:56). God truly is faithful!

The writer to the Hebrews defined faith as "being sure of what we hope for and certain of what we do not see" (Hebrews 11:1). The big problem for most people is that they tend to base everything on what the five senses reveal. And since the spiritual world is not subject to any of these, the faith of many people is often weak and impotent.

The eye of faith, however, perceives this unseen reality. The spiritual world is all around us, enclosing us, embracing us, altogether within our reach. God Himself is here awaiting our response to His presence—awaiting our response to His many promises. He is here to comfort us. We will become aware of the spiritual world the moment we begin to reckon upon its reality and believe what He has promised.

I often think about the story of Elisha in 2 Kings 6:8-23. Elisha was completely surrounded by enemy troops, yet he remained calm and relaxed. His servant, however, must have been climbing the walls at the sight of this hostile army with big, vicious-looking warriors and innumerable battle chariots on every side. (In my mind's eye, I picture this servant as being a Don Knotts type.) Undaunted, Elisha said to him: "Don't be afraid. Those who are with us are more than those who are with them" (6:16). Elisha then prayed to God, "'O LORD, open his eyes so he may see.' Then the LORD opened the servant's eyes, and he looked and saw the hills full of horses and chariots of fire all around Elisha" (6:17). God was protecting Elisha and his servant with a whole army of magnificent angelic beings!

Elisha never got frazzled because he was "sure of what he hoped for and certain of what he did not see." Here was a man who believed that God would fulfill what He had promised. The eyes of faith can see God acting on our behalf even when our physical eyes cannot. The eyes of faith recognize that God is indeed a God of promises and that He will respond to those who come to Him in faith!

Conditioning the Faith Muscle

Great Christian thinkers have often commented that faith is like a muscle. A muscle has to be repeatedly stretched to the limit of its endurance in order to build more strength. Without increased stress in training, the muscle will simply not grow.

In the same way, faith must be repeatedly tested to the limit of its endurance in order to expand and develop. Very often, God allows His children to go through trying experiences in order to develop their faith muscles (1 Peter 1:7). God's children need to learn to *trust* in the promises He has made. This learning process takes place in the school of real life—with all of its difficult trials and tribulations.

The book of Exodus shows this process in action. Following Israel's deliverance from Egypt, God first led them to Marah, a place where they would be *forced* to trust God to heal the water to make it drinkable. Significantly, God led them to Marah *before* leading them to Elim, a gorgeous oasis with plenty of good water (Exodus 15:22-27). God could have bypassed Marah altogether and brought them directly to Elim if He had wanted to. But, as is characteristic of God, He purposefully led them through the route that would yield maximum conditioning of their faith muscles, a route that forced them to trust in His promises of sustenance. God does the same type of thing with us. He often governs our circumstances so as to yield maximum conditioning of our faith muscles. God takes us through the school of hard knocks to teach us that He is reliable and that He indeed does faithfully follow through with His promises.

Faith and the Word of God

Without question, the Word of God can strengthen the faith of believers. John's Gospel proclaims that "these [things in John's Gospel] are written that you may believe" (John 20:31, insert added). Paul tells us that "faith comes from hearing the message, and the message is heard through the word of Christ" (Romans 10:17). If someone should ask, How can I increase my faith? the answer is, Saturate your mind with God's Word.

The more you know about the promises of God in the Word of God, the stronger your faith will be in appropriating them. Conversely, the less you know about the promises of God in His Word, the weaker your faith will be, and you will be ignorant of the vast and untapped reservoir of help that is available to you. No wonder the psalmist made a point of saying, "My eyes stay open through the watches of the night, that I may meditate on your promises" (Psalm 119:148).

My friend, I have compiled God's promises in this book so that...

- you may appropriate them in your life and enjoy the supernatural peace that goes along with trusting in these promises
- you may learn the lessons of faith and trust—and the accompanying blessings—that God has in store for you

May the Lord bless you mightily as you use this book!

Recognizing the Promises of God

If we are to place our faith in the promises of God, then at the outset, we must be sure what *is* and what is *not* a promise of God in the Bible. Obviously, if we claim a verse as a promise that is in fact not really a promise at all, then our faith is misplaced, and we will be disillusioned when we do not see the results we are looking for. We will not, however, be disappointed in God's Word so long as we interpret it correctly (2 Timothy 2:15) and claim as promises only those verses intended to be promises for us today.

On my bookshelf are a number of small paperback books containing "promises" of God. The problem is that many of the "promises" in these books are really not promises at all. For instance, one "promise" found in many of these books is 1 Thessalonians 4:9, found under the heading of "Brotherly Love": "Now about brotherly love we do not need to write to you, for you yourselves have been taught by God to love each other." In truth, this verse is simply affirming that the Thessalonian Christians have been taught by God to love one another. Nothing in this verse indicates that God is promising to do anything for believers. Claiming this verse as a promise is therefore a misuse of Scripture.

I could cite literally hundreds of such examples from various books that are full of Bible "promises," but such an exercise might seem ungracious and overly critical. My only point is that we need to be clear regarding what is and what is not a Bible promise. Only then can we confidently put our assurance in the Word of God.

Toward this end, I suggest some basic principles for understanding what is and what is not a Bible promise. These are simple observations based on many years of studying God's Word.

1. Promises made to *specific* individuals are not intended to be promises for *all* believers. An example is Genesis 12:2: "I will bless you; I will make your name great, and you will be a blessing." This promise was made to Abraham alone, not to believers in general. Therefore, modern believers should not claim this as a Bible promise for themselves.

Another example is 2 Kings 20:6: "I will add fifteen years to your life." This promise was made to Hezekiah alone, not to all believers.

When we encounter promises in the Bible, a good question to ask is: "Who is this promise being made to? Does the context indicate that it is a promise that I can claim, or is it a promise for a specific individual?"

2. Promises made to Old Testament Israelites are generally not promises to people today. Numerous Old Testament promises were made specifically to the Israelites in a very specific context and cannot be properly claimed by modern believers. In the book of Deuteronomy, for example, God through Moses promised great blessings if the theocratic (God-ruled) nation lived in obedience to the Sinaitic covenant God made with them. God also promised that if the nation disobeyed His commands, it would experience the punishments listed in the covenant—including exile from the land (Deuteronomy 28:15-68).

Old Testament history is replete with illustrations of how unfaithful Israel was to the covenant. The two most significant periods of exile for the Jewish people involved the fall of Israel to the Assyrians in 722 B.C. and the collapse of Judah to the Babylonians in 597–581 B.C. As God promised, disobedience brought exile to God's own people.

A rather famous promise made to the Old Testament Israelites that is sometimes misappropriated today is 2 Chronicles 7:14: "If my people, who are called by my name, will humble themselves and pray and seek my face and turn from their wicked ways, then will I hear from heaven and will forgive their sin and will heal their land." These are words that God spoke specifically to Solomon regarding the Israelites (God's "my people" of the Old Testament), yet how often do we hear people today claiming this verse as a promise from God regarding the United States? Now, don't get me wrong. Aside from being a *specific promise* to Israel, we also find in this verse the *general principle* that God responds to prayer and humility by bringing about healing. Based on this general principle, citizens of the United States should humble themselves and pray and ask God for the healing of our land—but we cannot claim this verse as an ironclad promise for the United States. To put it another way, the general principle can apply to all people and all nations—and God may well heal a modern nation that humbles itself and prays—but the ironclad promise that was set in stone and was guaranteed to be fulfilled was made to Israel alone.

Let us remember that we are instructed to avoid distorting the Bible (2 Peter 3:16) and that we are called to correctly handle the word of truth (2 Timothy 2:15). Because many verses in the Old Testament deal specifically with the Israelites in specific contexts, we would misinterpret the Bible if we claimed some of the promises for ourselves that God made to them. But we can derive principles from such promises and apply these principles to our situations. So, for example, when we read a promise made to the Israelite nation that God would bless their obedience (Deuteronomy 28:2), we can derive the general principle that God blesses obedience, and base our lives on that principle.

3. *Some* Bible promises made in the Old Testament *are* applicable to today. This would include Bible promises based on God's nature and not on specific circumstances among the Israelites. An example of this is Isaiah 55:11, which makes reference to the effectiveness of God's Word: "It will not return to me empty, but will accomplish what I desire and achieve the purpose for which I sent it." This promise is based entirely on God's intrinsic sovereignty. Since the verse is based on God's nature (a nature that does not change), the verse speaks of something that is true at all times in all places. Therefore, we may rest assured that God's Word is still as effective today as it was in Old Testament times.

Some promises made in the Old Testament are applicable today because of strong parallel promises in the New Testament. Such parallels indicate that God issues certain general promises to His people, regardless of whether they lived in Old Testament times or New Testament times and beyond. An example is Psalm 34:22: "No one will be condemned who takes refuge in him." This rings quite similar to John 3:18, where we read, "Whoever believes in him is not condemned."

Further, some Old Testament promises of God are made to those who "trust in the LORD" or "take refuge in the LORD" or "hope in the LORD," which are applicable to Christians today who trust in the Lord, take refuge in Him, and hope in Him. For example, in Isaiah 40:31 we read, "Those who hope in the LORD will renew their strength. They will soar on wings like eagles; they will run and not grow weary, they will walk and not be faint." In Psalm 31:23 we read that "the LORD preserves the faithful." In Psalm 34:10 we read that "those who seek the

LORD lack no good thing." Such general promises seem to belong to believers of all ages.

4. **"Wisdom sayings" in the book of Proverbs are not intended to be Bible promises.** The book of Proverbs is a "wisdom book" and contains maxims of moral wisdom. The maxims found in this book were engineered to help the young in ancient Israel acquire mental skills that promote wise living.

The word *proverb* literally means "to be like," or "to be compared with." A proverb, then, is a form of communicating truth by using comparisons or figures of speech. The proverbs, in a memorable way, crystallize and condense the writers' experiences and observations about life, and provide general principles that are generally (but not always) true. The reward of meditating on these maxims or "wisdom sayings" is, of course, wisdom. But these maxims were never intended as Bible promises.

A verse often misconstrued as a promise is Proverbs 22:6: "Train a child in the way he should go, and when he is old he will not turn from it." I know of parents who have claimed this verse as a promise and have done everything they could to bring their children up rightly and in the fear of the Lord. But in some cases, the children have ended up departing from Christianity and going astray in life. The parents of these children became disillusioned and wondered what they did wrong. But Proverbs 22:6 was never intended to be a promise. Like other "wisdom sayings" in the book of Proverbs, this verse contains a general principle that is generally true. But a general principle always involves some exceptions to the rule. (Keep in mind that God Himself is the most perfect parent there is, but His children, Adam and Eve, certainly went astray.)

The good news is that if you follow the general principles laid out in the book of Proverbs, you will generally see certain positive results in your life, and your life will generally be much more successful! But principles are not the same as promises.

5. **Words uttered by human beings that are recorded in Scripture are not necessarily Bible promises.** Of course, the words of the prophets and apostles *do* contain many promises of God, and we should pay careful attention to these promises. But in other cases, Scripture simply records something that a particular human being (who was not a prophet or an apostle) said, and those words cannot be

claimed as a promise. For example, in Job 4:8 we read: "Those who plow evil and those who sow trouble reap it." At first glance it might appear that God is promising to bring evil upon those who themselves cause evil. In context, however, these are words that Eliphaz the Temanite spoke to Job during his time of suffering. Therefore, these words do not constitute a promise of God. Likewise, in Job 8:6 we read: "If you are pure and upright, even now he will rouse himself on your behalf and restore you to your rightful place." Again, at first glance it might appear that God is here making a promise. But the context shows that these are words that Bildad the Shuhite spoke to Job. We must always be cautious not to claim as a promise of God something that a person spoke to another person.

6. Some Bible promises are unconditional, whereas others are conditional. This book contains both types of promises.

A conditional promise is a promise with an "if" attached. This type of promise necessitates meeting certain obligations or conditions before God fulfills it. If God's people fail in meeting the conditions, God is not obligated in any way to fulfill the promise. An example is James 1:25: "The man who looks intently into the perfect law that gives freedom, and continues to do this, not forgetting what he has heard, but doing it—he will be blessed in what he does." The promised blessing in this verse hinges on obeying God's Word. Another example is John 15:7: "If you remain in me and my words remain in you, ask whatever you wish, and it will be given you." This promise guarantees answered prayer *only* for those in whom Christ's words remain and those who remain in Christ. So long as the conditions are met, the promise is fulfilled.

An unconditional promise depends on no such conditions for its fulfillment. No "ifs" are attached. That which is promised is sovereignly given to the recipient of the promise apart from the recipient's merit (or lack of it). Such promises are true for all who belong to the family of God. Many of the promises relating to the Christian's positional standing in Christ or the blessings we have in Christ are unconditional. For example, we read in Galatians 4:6-7, "Because you are sons, God sent the Spirit of his Son into our hearts, the Spirit who calls out, '*Abba,* Father.' So you are no longer a slave, but a son; and since you are a son, God has made you also an heir." The fact that we are sons and heirs in God's family does not hinge on meeting certain conditions. Rather it is something that is true of all Christians.

7. **When interpreting the promises of God, always keep in mind what other Scriptures on the same subject reveal.** Scripture interprets Scripture. This principle says that if one interprets a particular verse in a way that clearly contradicts other Bible verses, then one's interpretation is incorrect. Scriptural harmony is essential. In view of this principle, consider the Bible promise in Mark 11:23-24: "I tell you the truth, if anyone says to this mountain, 'Go, throw yourself into the sea,' and does not doubt in his heart but believes that what he says will happen, it will be done for him. Therefore I tell you, whatever you ask for in prayer, believe that you have received it, and it will be yours."

We must interpret this promise in light of what other Scripture verses reveal. The broader context of Scripture places limitations on what God will give. God cannot literally give us anything. Some things are actually impossible for God to give. For example, God cannot grant a request of a creature to be God. Neither can He answer a request to approve of our sin. God will not give us a stone if we ask for bread, nor will He give us a snake if we ask for fish (Matthew 7:9-10).

Scripture places other conditions on God's promise to answer prayer in addition to faith. We must abide in Him and let His Word abide in us (John 15:7 KJV). We cannot "ask amiss" out of our own selfishness (James 4:3 KJV). Furthermore, we must ask "according to his will" (1 John 5:14). We must ever keep in mind that when we claim God's conditional promises, this "if it be your will" must always be stated or implied.

Most Bibles today have cross-references listed in the side column. When reading a Bible promise, I recommend that you look up some of the cross-references to make sure you are interpreting the promise rightly.

8. When interpreting the promises of God, let the context determine the proper meaning of biblical words. I'll illustrate my point with 2 Corinthians 8:9: "For you know the grace of our Lord Jesus Christ, that though He was rich, yet for your sake He became poor, so that you through His poverty might become rich." Some have claimed this verse as a promise of financial prosperity. Yet, this understanding of the verse does not fit the context. Notice that if Paul was intending to say that financial prosperity is provided for in the atonement, he was offering the Corinthians something that he himself did not possess at the time. Indeed, in 1 Corinthians 4:11 (NASB) Paul informed these same individuals that he was "hungry and thirsty," "poorly clothed," and "homeless." Contextually, it seems clear that 2 Corinthians 8:9 is speaking about *spiritual* prosperity, not financial prosperity. This fits both the immediate context in 2 Corinthians and the broader context of Paul's other writings.

Another illustration might be found in Isaiah 53:5: "He was pierced for our transgressions, he was crushed for our iniquities...by his wounds we are healed." Some have claimed this verse as a promise of physical healing, but spiritual healing of the sin problem seems to be in view. The Hebrew word for healing *(napha)* can refer not only to physical healing but also to spiritual healing. The context of Isaiah 53:4-5 points to spiritual healing. After all, "transgressions" and "iniquities" set the context for what is "healed." Further, numerous verses in Scripture substantiate the view that physical healing in mortal life is not guaranteed in the atonement and that it is not always God's will to heal. The apostle Paul couldn't heal Timothy's stomach problem (1 Timothy 5:23) nor could he heal Trophimus at Miletus (2 Timothy 4:20) or Epaphroditus (Philippians 2:25-27). Paul spoke of "a bodily illness" he had (Galatians 4:13-15 NASB). He also suffered a "thorn in the flesh" which God allowed him to retain (2 Corinthians 12:7-9). God certainly allowed Job to go through a time of physical suffering (Job 1–2). In none of these cases did these individuals act as if they thought their healing was promised in the atonement. They accepted their situations and trusted in God's grace for sustenance.

Here is a review of the principles we have discussed:

Principles for Interpreting Bible Promises

1. Promises made to *specific* individuals are not intended to be promises for *all* believers.
2. Promises made to Old Testament Israelites are generally not promises to people today.
3. *Some* Bible promises made in the Old Testament *are* applicable to today. These would include promises based on God's nature, promises with New Testament parallels, and general promises to "those who trust in the Lord."
4. "Wisdom sayings" in the book of Proverbs are not intended to be Bible promises.
5. Words uttered by human beings that are recorded in Scripture are not necessarily Bible promises.
6. Some Bible promises are unconditional, whereas others are conditional.
7. When interpreting the promises of God, always keep in mind what other Scriptures on the same subject reveal.
8. When interpreting the promises of God, let the context determine the proper meaning of biblical words.

When Life Throws You a Punch...

The fact that God has given us many wonderful promises in the Bible is not a guarantee that our lives will be without pain or difficult circumstances. Among the biblical saints who suffered are Job (Job 1–2), the apostle Paul (2 Corinthians 12:9), Timothy (1 Timothy 5:23), Epaphroditus (Philippians 2:25-27), and Trophimus (2 Timothy 4:20). Christians who believe in the promises of God will still get sick, will go through trials and tribulations, and may even encounter tragedy. As we read in the book of Job, "Man is born to trouble as surely as sparks fly upward" (Job 5:7), and "Man born of woman is of few days and full of trouble" (Job 14:1).

But the good news is that we are never alone in troublesome situations. The God of promises is always there to see us through (Psalm 46:1; 50:15). And, very often, it is the very promises of God that enable us to patiently endure through our difficult circumstances (2 Peter 1:4).

Having said that, I now invite you to drink richly from the promises of God in the following pages. May the Lord encourage you and bless you through these promises!

How to Use This Book

This book includes two special features.

First, to help you quickly find the verse you need, I've included a concise heading along with each promise. The book is much easier to use this way.

Second, under most (not all) verse citations, I provide insights on key Hebrew and Greek words so you'll be sure to interpret the verse correctly. (Not all verses need insights from the Greek or Hebrew.) For illustration purposes, consider John 15:10-11:

Obey Christ, and you will experience joy

If you *obey* my commands, you will *remain* in my love, just as I have *obeyed* my Father's commands and *remain* in his love. I have told you this so that my *joy* may be in you and that your *joy* may be *complete.*

—John 15:10-11

obey—keep, guard, observe
remain—stay, live, dwell, abide
joy—rejoicing, happiness, gladness
complete—made full

Notice three things:

- The top heading summarizes the promise.
- The italicized words in the verse point you to the word list below the verse.
- The words listed below the verse contain insights from the Greek.

The Promises of God from A to Z

A

Abiding in Christ

Obey Christ, and you will experience joy

If you *obey* my commands, you will *remain* in my love, just as I have *obeyed* my Father's commands and *remain* in his love. I have told you this so that my *joy* may be in you and that your *joy* may be *complete.*

—JOHN 15:10-11

obey—keep, guard, observe
remain—stay, live, dwell, abide
joy—rejoicing, happiness, gladness
complete—made full

Abiding in Christ yields fruit

If a man *remains* in me and I in him, he will bear much fruit; apart from me you can do *nothing.*

—JOHN 15:5

remains—abides, lives, dwells
nothing—nothing at all, nothing in any way

> God's promises are like the stars;
> the darker the night
> the brighter they shine.
>
> *David Nicholas*

A

God's love is made complete in the one who abides

If anyone *obeys* his word, God's love is truly made *complete* in him. This is how we know we are in him: Whoever claims to *live* in him must *walk* as Jesus did.

—1 JOHN 2:5-6

obeys—keeps, guards, observes
complete—perfect
live—abide, remain
walk—conduct one's life

Acceptance

Christ will never reject any who come to Him

All that the Father gives me will come to me, and whoever comes to me I will never *drive away.*

—JOHN 6:37

drive away—send out, expel

God will draw near to those who draw near to Him

Come near to God and he will come near to you.

—JAMES 4:8

God provides absolute proof of His love for us

God *demonstrates* his own *love* for us in this: While we were still *sinners*, Christ died for us.

—ROMANS 5:8

demonstrates—proves
love—active love
sinners—complete moral failures

God cleanses the stain of sin from your soul

"Come now, let us reason together," says the LORD. "Though your *sins* are like scarlet, they shall be as *white* as snow; though they are red as crimson, they shall be like wool."

—ISAIAH 1:18

sins—actions contrary to the law of God
white—spotless, purified

We are brought near through Christ

In Christ Jesus you who once were *far away* have been brought near through the blood of Christ.

—EPHESIANS 2:13

far away—a long way off, distant

We are recipients of salvation, not wrath

God did not appoint us to suffer *wrath* but to receive *salvation* through our Lord Jesus Christ.

—1 THESSALONIANS 5:9

wrath—anger, displeasure, hostility
salvation—rescue, deliverance

Those who trust in Jesus are saved from wrath

Since we have now been *justified* by his blood, how much more shall we be *saved* from God's *wrath* through him!

—ROMANS 5:9

justified—declared righteous
saved—rescued, delivered
wrath—anger, displeasure, hostility

A

God completely removes sin from His children

As far as the east is from the west, so far has he *removed* our *transgressions* from us.

—PSALM 103:12

removed—driven far away
transgressions—sins, rebellious acts

Adoption

Those who believe in Jesus are God's children

To all who received him, to those who *believed in* his name, he gave the *right* to become children of God.

—JOHN 1:12

believed in—put trust in, relied on
right—authority, power

You are all *sons* of God through *faith in* Christ Jesus.

—GALATIANS 3:26

sons—endeared children
faith in—belief in, trust in

We are members of God's household

You are no longer foreigners and aliens, but fellow citizens with God's people and members of God's *household.*

—EPHESIANS 2:19

household—immediate family

Because of God's love, we are His children

How great is the *love* the Father has lavished on us, that we should be called children of God! And that is what we are!

—1 JOHN 3:1

love—active love

We are not slaves but God's children with an inheritance

Because you are *sons*, God sent the Spirit of his Son into our hearts, the Spirit who calls out, "*Abba*, Father." So you are no longer a slave, but a son; and since you are a son, God has made you also an heir.

—GALATIANS 4:6-7

sons—endeared children
Abba—dear daddy

> Oh, it is sad for a poor Christian
> to stand at the door of the promise
> in the dark night of affliction,
> afraid to draw the latch!
>
> *William Gurnall*

We are not slaves to fear but God's children

Those who are led by the Spirit of God are *sons* of God. For you did not receive a spirit that makes you *a slave* again to fear, but you received the Spirit of *sonship*. And by him we cry, "*Abba*, Father."

—ROMANS 8:14-15

sons—endeared children
a slave—in bondage
sonship—an adopted child with an inheritance
Abba—dear daddy

God's children are conformed to the likeness of Jesus

Those God *foreknew* he also *predestined* to be conformed to the *likeness* of his Son, that he might be the firstborn among many brothers.

—ROMANS 8:29

foreknew—knew beforehand
predestined—decided beforehand
likeness—image, portrait

God will lovingly discipline His children

The Lord *disciplines* those he loves, and he *punishes* everyone he accepts as a *son. Endure* hardship as discipline; God is treating you as *sons.*

—HEBREWS 12:6-7

disciplines—instructs, educates, trains
punishes—scourges, chastises
son—endeared child
endure—stand firm, persevere

Aging and Dying

God is our guide to the very end of our lives

This God is our God for ever and ever; he will be our guide even to the *end.*

—PSALM 48:14

end—death

Our bodies may age, but our spirits are renewed

We do not *lose heart.* Though outwardly we are *wasting away*, yet inwardly we are *being renewed* day by day.

—2 CORINTHIANS 4:16

lose heart—give up, become discouraged, become wearied
wasting away—progressively decaying
being renewed—continually and perpetually renewed

God will abolish death

He will *swallow up* death forever. The Sovereign LORD will *wipe away* the tears from all faces.

—ISAIAH 25:8

swallow up—consume, devour, gulp down
wipe away—blot out, exterminate

Death will be swallowed up in victory

When the perishable has been clothed with the imperishable, and the mortal with immortality, then the saying that is written will come true: "Death has been *swallowed up* in victory."

—1 CORINTHIANS 15:54

swallowed up—overwhelmed, drowned

Permanent resurrection bodies await us

We know that if the earthly tent we live in is *destroyed*, we have a building from God, an eternal house in heaven, not built by human hands.

—2 CORINTHIANS 5:1

destroyed—thrown down, dissolved, abolished

Anger

Unrighteous anger brings judgment

I tell you that anyone who is *angry* with his brother will be subject to judgment. Again, anyone who says to his brother, "*Raca*," is answerable to the Sanhedrin. But anyone who says, "You fool!" will be in danger of the fire of hell.

—MATTHEW 5:22

angry—enraged, hostile
Raca—empty-headed one (insult)

God will avenge us

Do not *take revenge*, my friends, but leave room for God's *wrath*, for it is written: "It is mine to *avenge*; I will repay," says the Lord.

—ROMANS 12:19 (see also HEBREWS 10:30)

take revenge—avenge yourselves, get your own justice
wrath—righteous anger, displeasure, hostility
avenge—punish, bring justice

God's anger is short-lived

His anger lasts only a moment, but his *favor* lasts a lifetime; weeping may remain for a night, but *rejoicing* comes in the morning.

—PSALM 30:5

favor—pleasure, acceptance
rejoicing—a shout of joy, a song of joy

Anxiety

The Lord sustains us in our troubles

Cast your *cares* on the LORD and he will *sustain* you; he will never let the righteous fall.

—PSALM 55:22

cast—throw, hurl
cares—burdens
sustain—uphold, support, bear up

God is the source of perfect peace

Do not be *anxious* about anything, but in everything, by prayer and *petition*, with thanksgiving, present your requests to God. And the *peace* of God, which *transcends* all understanding, will *guard* your hearts and your minds in Christ Jesus.

—PHILIPPIANS 4:6-7

anxious—worried, concerned
petition—definite requests
peace—tranquility, serenity
transcends—surpasses, exceeds
guard—shield

Christ gives us peace

Peace I leave with you; my *peace* I give you. I do not give to you as the world gives. Do not let your hearts be *troubled* and do not be *afraid.*

—JOHN 14:27

peace—tranquility, a sense of welfare
troubled—disturbed, terrified, thrown into confusion
afraid—timid, cowardly

I have told you these things, so that in me you may have *peace.* In this world you will have *trouble.* But take heart! I have *overcome* the world.

—JOHN 16:33

peace—tranquility, a sense of welfare, with no fears
trouble—distress, tribulation, oppression
overcome—conquered, triumphed, overpowered

Christ gives us rest

Come to me, all you who are *weary* and *burdened,* and I will give you *rest.*

—MATTHEW 11:28

weary—tired, labored
burdened—weighted down
rest—refreshment, relief

Even in our troubles, God works for our good

We know that in all things God works for the *good* of those who *love* him, who have been called according to his purpose.

—ROMANS 8:28

good—positive good, moral good
love—actively love

A

Assurance of Salvation

God's people will never perish

My sheep *listen to* my voice; I know them, and they follow me. I give them eternal life, and they shall *never* perish; no one can *snatch* them out of my hand. My Father, who has given them to me, is greater than all; no one can *snatch* them out of my Father's hand.

—John 10:27-29

listen to—understand, obey, pay attention to
never—never by any means
snatch—steal, carry off

God's people are sealed by the Holy Spirit

Having believed, you were *marked* in him with a *seal*, the promised Holy Spirit, who is a *deposit* guaranteeing our inheritance until the redemption of those who are God's possession.

—Ephesians 1:13-14 (see also Ephesians 4:30)

marked—stamped
seal—mark of possession, mark of identity
deposit—downpayment, pledge, foretaste

> The sacred promises, though in themselves most sure and precious, are of no avail for the comfort and sustenance of the soul unless you grasp them by faith, plead them in prayer, expect them by hope, and receive them with gratitude.
>
> *Charles Haddon Spurgeon*

Atonement

We are redeemed and forgiven

In him we have *redemption* through his blood, the *forgiveness* of sins, in accordance with the riches of God's *grace.*

—EPHESIANS 1:7

redemption—ransom, release from sin
forgiveness—pardon, cancellation of all debt
grace—unmerited favor, kindness

We are forgiven

He *forgave us* all our sins, having *canceled* the written code, with its regulations, that was against us and that stood opposed to us; he took it away, nailing it to the cross.

—COLOSSIANS 2:13-14

forgave us—canceled the debt of
canceled—blotted out, wiped away

We are saved from God's wrath

Since we have now been *justified* by his blood, how much more shall we be *saved* from God's *wrath* through him!

—ROMANS 5:9

justified—declared righteous
saved—rescued, delivered
wrath—anger, displeasure, hostility

Jesus died for the sins of the world

He is the *atoning sacrifice* for our *sins,* and not only for ours but also for the *sins* of the whole world.

—1 JOHN 2:2

atoning sacrifice—propitiation, basis of forgiveness
sins—wrongdoings, acts contrary to God's law

B

Jesus' sacrifice takes away our sins

Christ was sacrificed once to take away the *sins* of many people; and he will appear a second time, not to bear sin, but to bring *salvation* to those who are waiting for him.

—HEBREWS 9:28

sins—wrongdoings, acts contrary to God's law
salvation—final rescue, ultimate deliverance

B

Backsliding

God can deliver you from any temptation

No *temptation* has *seized* you except what is common to man. And God is faithful; he will not let you be tempted beyond what you can *bear*. But when you are tempted, he will also provide a *way out* so that you can *stand up* under it.

—1 CORINTHIANS 10:13

temptation—trial, enticement to sin
seized—laid hold of, overtaken
bear—endure, resist
way out—means of escape
stand up—endure, bear up

Dependence on the Holy Spirit brings victory

Live by the Spirit, and you will not *gratify* the desires of the sinful nature.

—GALATIANS 5:16

live by—habitually walk in dependence on
gratify—fulfill, give in to

Those who believe in Jesus overcome the world

Everyone born of God *overcomes* the world. This is the victory that has *overcome* the world, even our faith. Who is it that *overcomes* the world? Only he who believes that Jesus is the Son of God.

—1 JOHN 5:4-5

overcomes—triumphs over, overpowers, conquers

God forgives and cleanses us if we confess

If we *confess* our sins, he is *faithful* and *just* and will *forgive* us our sins and *purify* us from all unrighteousness.

—1 JOHN 1:9

confess—admit, agree, acknowledge
faithful—trustworthy, reliable
just—upright, righteous
forgive—pardon, remit, cancel
purify—cleanse, make clean

God gives the crown of life to those who persevere

Blessed is the man who *perseveres* under trial, because when he has stood the test, he will receive the crown of life that God has promised to those who love him.

—JAMES 1:12

perseveres—stands firm, endures

Belief

Faith in God brings big results

Everything is possible for him who *believes.*

—MARK 9:23

believes—trusts, has faith

B

Those who believe in Jesus receive eternal life

For God so *loved* the world that he gave his one and only Son, that whoever *believes in* him shall not *perish* but have eternal life.

—JOHN 3:16 (see also ACTS 10:43; 16:31)

loved—actively loved, intensely loved
believes in—trusts in, puts faith in, relies on
perish—come to destruction

Whoever *believes in* the Son has eternal life, but whoever rejects the Son will not see life, for God's *wrath* remains on him.

—JOHN 3:36 (see also JOHN 3:18; 6:47)

believes in—trusts in, puts faith in, relies on
wrath—anger, displeasure, hostility

Those who believe in Jesus are spiritually satisfied

Jesus declared, "I am the bread of life. He who comes to me will *never* go hungry, and he who *believes in* me will never be thirsty."

—JOHN 6:35

never—absolutely never
believes in—trusts in, puts faith in, relies on

Those who believe in Jesus will not remain in darkness

I have come into the world as a light, so that no one who *believes in* me should stay in darkness.

—JOHN 12:46

believes in—trusts in, puts faith in, relies on

Those who believe in Jesus will be resurrected

Jesus said to her, "I am the resurrection and the life. He who *believes in* me will live, even though he dies; and whoever lives and *believes in* me will never die."

—JOHN 11:25-26

believes in—trusts in, puts faith in, relies on

Benevolence

God gives you all you need to do good

God is able to make all *grace abound* to you, so that in all things at all times, having all that you need, you will *abound* in every good work.

—2 CORINTHIANS 9:8

grace—unmerited favor, kindness

abound—overflow, brim over

God will not forget your good work

God is not unjust; he will not forget your work and the *love* you have shown him as you have *helped* his people and continue to help them.

—HEBREWS 6:10

love—active love

helped—attended to, waited upon, served

Give secretly, and God will reward you

When you *give* to the needy, do not let your left hand know what your right hand is doing, so that your giving may be in *secret.* Then your Father, who sees what is done in *secret,* will reward you.

—MATTHEW 6:3-4

give—charitably give, freely give

secret—hidden, unseen, undisclosed

Doing good to others is doing good to Christ

B

I tell you the truth, whatever you did for one of the *least* of these brothers of mine, you did for me.

—MATTHEW 25:40

least—most trivial, least significant

> God is the God of promise. He keeps his word, even when that seems impossible; even when the circumstances seem to point to the opposite.
>
> *Colin Urquhart*

God blesses those who help the weak

Blessed is he who has regard for the *weak*; the LORD *delivers* him in times of trouble. The LORD will *protect* him and preserve his life.

—PSALM 41:1-2

blessed—happy, joyful, favored by God
weak—poor, needy, scrawny
delivers—saves, rescues
protect—guard, watch over

Bereavement

The death of Christians is precious to God

Precious in the sight of the LORD is the death of his *saints.*

—PSALM 116:15

precious—important, valuable
saints—holy ones, godly ones

God comforts those who mourn

Blessed are those who *mourn,* for they will be *comforted.*

—MATTHEW 5:4

blessed—happy, joyful, favored by God
mourn—grieve
comforted—encouraged, exhorted

God will abolish tears and death

He will *wipe* every tear from their eyes. There will be *no more* death or mourning or crying or pain, for the old order of things has passed away.

—REVELATION 21:4

wipe—blot out, exterminate
no more—absolutely no more

A wonderful destiny awaits those who love God

No eye has *seen,* no ear has heard, no mind has conceived what God has prepared for those who *love* him.

—1 CORINTHIANS 2:9

seen—perceived
love—actively love

Permanent resurrection bodies await us

We know that if the earthly tent we live in is *destroyed,* we have a building from God, an eternal house in heaven, not built by human hands.

—2 CORINTHIANS 5:1

destroyed—thrown down, dissolved, abolished

We will be resurrected

I am the resurrection and the life. He who *believes in* me will live, even though he dies.

—JOHN 11:25

believes in—trusts in, puts faith in, relies on

Bible

God's Word endures forever

Heaven and earth will *pass away*, but my words will never *pass away*.

—MARK 13:31

pass away—disappear, come to an end

God's Word is powerfully effective

It will not return to me *empty*, but will accomplish what I *desire* and *achieve* the purpose for which I sent it.

—ISAIAH 55:11

empty—empty-handed, without satisfaction
desire—delight in, take pleasure in
achieve—prevail, succeed, be victorious

Scripture is inspired and equips us

All Scripture is *God-breathed* and is *useful* for teaching, rebuking, correcting and training in righteousness, so that the man of God may be *thoroughly equipped* for every good work.

—2 TIMOTHY 3:16-17

God-breathed—inspired
useful—valuable, profitable
thoroughly equipped—capable of meeting all demands, fully proficient

God's Word revives the soul

The law of the LORD is *perfect, reviving* the soul. The statutes of the LORD are trustworthy, making wise the simple. The precepts of the LORD are right, giving *joy* to the heart. The commands of the LORD are radiant, giving light to the eyes.

—PSALM 19:7-8

perfect—blameless, without defect
reviving—recovering, restoring
joy—rejoicing, delight

Tampering with God's Word brings judgment

I *warn* everyone who hears the words of the prophecy of this book: If anyone adds anything to them, God will add to him the *plagues* described in this book. And if anyone takes words away from this book of prophecy, God will take away from him his share in the tree of life and in the holy city, which are described in this book.

—REVELATION 22:18-19

warn—testify, vow to
plagues—punishment, flogging, wounding

Blessing

Those who trust the Lord are blessed

Blessed is the man who *trusts in* the LORD, whose *confidence* is in him.

—JEREMIAH 17:7

trusts in—relies on, puts confidence in
confidence—security, firm trust

Those who fear the Lord are blessed

Blessed are all who fear the LORD, who *walk* in his ways.

—PSALM 128:1

walk—conduct their lives

The poor in spirit are blessed

Blessed are the *poor in spirit,* for theirs is the kingdom of heaven.

—MATTHEW 5:3

blessed—happy, joyful, favored by God
poor in spirit—humble

Those who mourn are blessed

Blessed are those who *mourn,* for they will be *comforted.*

—MATTHEW 5:4

blessed—happy, joyful, favored by God
mourn—grieve
comforted—encouraged, exhorted

> Learn to put your hand on all spiritual blessings in Christ and say "Mine."
>
> *F.B. Meyer*

The meek are blessed

Blessed are the *meek,* for they will inherit the earth.

—MATTHEW 5:5

blessed—happy, joyful, favored by God
meek—gentle, humble

Those who yearn for righteousness are blessed

Blessed are those who hunger and thirst for righteousness, for they will be *filled.*

—MATTHEW 5:6

blessed—happy, joyful, favored by God
filled—filled to satisfaction, filled to the full

The merciful are blessed

Blessed are *the merciful,* for they will be shown mercy.

—MATTHEW 5:7

blessed—happy, joyful, favored by God
the merciful—the compassionate, those who show pity

The pure in heart are blessed

Blessed are the *pure* in heart, for they will see God.

—MATTHEW 5:8

blessed—happy, joyful, favored by God
pure—clean, innocent

The peacemakers are blessed

Blessed are the *peacemakers,* for they will be called sons of God.

—MATTHEW 5:9

blessed—happy, joyful, favored by God
peacemakers—reconcilers

Those persecuted because of righteousness are blessed

B *Blessed* are those who are *persecuted* because of righteousness, for theirs is the kingdom of heaven.

—MATTHEW 5:10

blessed—happy, joyful, favored by God
persecuted—harassed, oppressed

Blessed are you when people *insult* you, *persecute* you and falsely say all kinds of evil against you because of me. Rejoice and be glad, because great is your reward in heaven.

—MATTHEW 5:11-12

blessed—happy, joyful, favored by God
insult—denounce, rebuke
persecute—harass, oppress

Blood of Jesus

We are redeemed and forgiven

In him we have *redemption* through his blood, the *forgiveness* of sins, in accordance with the riches of God's *grace.*

—EPHESIANS 1:7

redemption—ransom, release from sin
forgiveness—pardon, cancellation of all debt
grace—unmerited favor, kindness

We are redeemed

It was not with *perishable* things such as silver or gold that you were redeemed from the *empty* way of life handed down to you from your forefathers, but with the *precious* blood of Christ, a lamb without blemish or defect.

—1 PETER 1:18-19

perishable—that which does not last
empty—futile, worthless
precious—costly, valuable

We are purified from all sin

If we *walk* in the light, as he is in the light, we have *fellowship* with one another, and the blood of Jesus, his Son, purifies us from all sin.

—1 JOHN 1:7

walk—conduct our lives
fellowship—sharing

Our consciences are cleansed

How much more, then, will the blood of Christ, who through the eternal Spirit offered himself unblemished to God, *cleanse* our consciences from acts that lead to death, so that we may serve the living God!

—HEBREWS 9:14

cleanse—purify, make clean

Boldness

God is always faithful to us

Let us hold *unswervingly* to the *hope* we profess, for he who promised is *faithful.*

—HEBREWS 10:23

unswervingly—without wavering
hope—expectation
faithful—trustworthy, reliable

God is always for us

If God is for us, who can *be against* us? He who did not spare his own Son, but gave him up for us all—how will he not also, along with him, *graciously* give us all things?

—ROMANS 8:31-32

be against—successfully be against
graciously—freely

We can be confident in approaching God

This is the *confidence* we have in approaching God: that if we ask anything according to his will, he hears us. And if we *know* that he hears us—whatever we ask—we *know* that we have what we asked of him.

—1 JOHN 5:14-15

confidence—bold assurance
know—know with certainty and assurance

We are conquerors in Christ

In all these things we are *more than conquerors* through him who *loved* us.

—ROMANS 8:37

more than conquerors—complete in our conquest
loved—actively loved

Those who trust in Jesus are empowered

I tell you the truth, anyone who has *faith in* me will do what I have been doing. He will do even greater things than these, because I am going to the Father.

—JOHN 14:12

faith in—trust in, belief in, reliance upon

Burdens

The Lord sustains us in our troubles

Cast your *cares* on the LORD and he will *sustain* you; he will never let the righteous fall.

—PSALM 55:22

cast—throw, hurl
cares—burdens
sustain—uphold, support, bear up

Christ gives us rest

Come to me, all you who are *weary* and *burdened*, and I will give you *rest.*

—MATTHEW 11:28

weary—tired, labored
burdened—weighted down
rest—refreshment, relief

Turning anxieties over to God yields perfect peace

Do not be *anxious* about anything, but in everything, by prayer and *petition*, with thanksgiving, present your requests to God. And the *peace* of God, which *transcends* all understanding, will *guard* your hearts and your minds in Christ Jesus.

—PHILIPPIANS 4:6-7

anxious—worried, concerned, fretful
petition—definite requests
peace—tranquility, sense of welfare, fearing nothing
transcends—surpasses, exceeds
guard—shield

Have faith in God, my heart,
Trust and be unafraid;
God will fulfill in every part
Each promise he has made.

Bryn Austin Rees

God is our refuge and strength

God is our *refuge* and *strength*, an ever-present *help* in trouble.

—PSALM 46:1

refuge—shelter
strength—stronghold, fortification
help—support, ally

C

Care

God cares for us and will meet all our needs

My God will *meet* all your needs according to his glorious riches in Christ Jesus.

—PHILIPPIANS 4:19

meet—liberally fulfill, complete

God will take care of our earthly needs

Do not *worry* about your life, what you will eat or drink; or about your body, what you will wear. Is not life more important than food, and the body more important than clothes? Look at the birds of the air; they do not sow or reap or store away in barns, and yet your heavenly Father feeds them. Are you not much more valuable than they?

—MATTHEW 6:25-26

worry—have anxiety, be concerned, be fretful

The Lord will take care of us in our troubles

Cast your *cares* on the LORD and he will *sustain* you; he will never let the righteous fall.

—PSALM 55:22

cast—throw, hurl

cares—burdens

sustain—uphold, support, bear up

Carnality

The Holy Spirit empowers us to overcome sinful desires

Live by the Spirit, and you will not *gratify* the *desires* of the sinful nature.

—GALATIANS 5:16

live—habitually conduct your life
gratify—fulfill, give in to
desires—cravings

Pleasing the Holy Spirit yields eternal life

The one who sows to please his sinful nature, from that nature will *reap destruction*; the one who sows to please the Spirit, from the Spirit will *reap* eternal life.

—GALATIANS 6:8

reap—harvest
destruction—corruption, depravity

The mind controlled by the Spirit is life and peace

Those who *live according to* the sinful nature have their minds set on what that nature desires; but those who live in accordance with the Spirit have their minds set on what the Spirit desires. The mind of sinful man is death, but the mind controlled by the Spirit is life and *peace*.

—ROMANS 8:5-6

live according to—are controlled by
peace—tranquility, serenity

Character

God abundantly blesses a righteous character

The LORD God is a sun and shield; the LORD bestows favor and honor; no good thing does he withhold from those whose walk is *blameless.*

—PSALM 84:11

blameless—unblemished, without defect

Those who yearn for righteousness will be satisfied

Blessed are those who hunger and thirst for righteousness, for they will be *filled.*

—MATTHEW 5:6

blessed—happy, joyful, favored by God
filled—filled to satisfaction, filled to the full

Righteousness yields peace and confidence

The fruit of righteousness will be *peace*; the effect of righteousness will be quietness and *confidence* forever.

—ISAIAH 32:17

peace—well-being, contentment
confidence—security, safety

Charity

God will bless you if you bless others

Give, and it will be given to you. A good measure, pressed down, shaken together and running over, will be poured into your lap. For with the measure you use, it will be measured to you.

—LUKE 6:38

Give secretly, and God will bless you

When you give to the needy, do not let your left hand know what your right hand is doing, so that your giving may be *in secret.* Then your Father, who sees what is done in secret, will *reward* you.

—MATTHEW 6:3-4

in secret—unseen, hidden, undisclosed

reward—pay back openly

God will reward us for charity to the disenfranchised

When you give a banquet, invite the poor, the crippled, the lame, the blind, and you will be *blessed.* Although they cannot repay you, you will be repaid at the resurrection of the righteous.

—LUKE 14:13-14

blessed—happy, joyful, receiving God's favor

Charitable kindness to children brings blessing

If anyone gives even a cup of cold water to one of these little ones because he is my disciple, I tell you the truth, he will *certainly not* lose his *reward.*

—MATTHEW 10:42

certainly not—absolutely not

reward—that which is paid pack

God's promise is better than any bond or note on any bank, financial institution, or most stable government, for all these may have to repudiate their bond; God never does so.

R.C.H. Lenski

God blesses those who help the weak

Blessed is he who has regard for the *weak*; the LORD *delivers* him in times of trouble. The LORD will *protect* him and preserve his life.

—PSALM 41:1-2

blessed—happy, joyful, favored by God
weak—poor, needy, scrawny
delivers—saves, rescues
protect—guard, watch over

Charity to others is charity to Christ

I tell you the truth, whatever you did for one of the *least* of these brothers of mine, you did for me.

—MATTHEW 25:40

least—most trivial, least significant

Children

Little children are welcome in God's kingdom

Let the little children come to me, and do not *hinder* them, for the kingdom of heaven belongs to such as these.

—MATTHEW 19:14 (see also MARK 10:14-16)

hinder—restrain, forbid, oppress

Everyone is offered the blessing of salvation

Repent and be baptized, every one of you, in the name of Jesus Christ for the *forgiveness* of your sins. And you will receive the gift of the Holy Spirit. The promise is for you and your children and for all who are far off—for all whom the Lord our God will call.

—ACTS 2:38-39

repent—change your mind, change your attitudes
forgiveness—pardon, cancellation of debt

Obedience to parents yields longevity

Children, obey your parents in the Lord, for this is *right.* "*Honor* your father and mother"—which is the first commandment with a promise—"that it may go well with you and that you may enjoy long life on the earth."

—EPHESIANS 6:1-3 (see also COLOSSIANS 3:20)

right—righteous, upright

honor—show respect for, give recognition to, esteem, show value for

God blesses the children of righteous parents

From everlasting to everlasting the LORD's *love* is with those who *fear* him, and his righteousness with their children's children.

—PSALM 103:17

love—loyal love, faithful devotion

fear—worshipfully fear, show reverence to

Becoming humble like a child yields greatness

Whoever *humbles* himself like this child is the greatest in the kingdom of heaven.

—MATTHEW 18:4

humbles—brings low

Children of God

Those who believe in Jesus are God's children

To all who received him, to those who *believed in* his name, he gave the *right* to become children of God.

—JOHN 1:12

believed in—put trust in, relied upon

right—authority, power

We become God's children through faith in Jesus

You are all *sons* of God through *faith* in Christ Jesus.

—GALATIANS 3:26

sons—endeared children

faith—belief, trust

God's children are not slaves to fear

Those who are led by the Spirit of God are *sons* of God. For you did not receive a spirit that makes you *a slave* again to fear, but you received the Spirit of sonship. And by him we cry, "*Abba*, Father."

—ROMANS 8:14-15 (see also GALATIANS 4:6-7)

sons—endeared children

a slave—in bondage

Abba—dear daddy

As God's children, we are heirs of God

The Spirit himself *testifies* with our spirit that we are God's children. Now if we are children, then we are heirs—heirs of God and co-heirs with Christ, if indeed we share in his sufferings in order that we may also share in his glory.

—ROMANS 8:16-17

testifies—confirms

As children of God, our future is glorious

Dear friends, now we are children of God, and what we will be has not yet been *made known*. But we know that when he appears, we shall be *like* him, for we shall *see* him as he is.

—1 JOHN 3:2

made known—disclosed, revealed

like—similar to

see—perceive

Christ's Return

Jesus will come again physically and visibly

This same Jesus, who has been *taken* from you into heaven, will come back in the *same way* you have seen him go into heaven.

—ACTS 1:11

taken—lifted up, brought up

same way—same manner (visibly and physically)

Every eye will witness the Second Coming

Look, he is coming with the clouds, and every eye will *see* him, even those who pierced him; and all the peoples of the earth will *mourn* because of him.

—REVELATION 1:7

see—perceive, notice

mourn—beat the breast in mourning

Christ will come at an hour we do not expect

You also must be *ready*, because the Son of Man will come at an hour when you do not expect him.

—LUKE 12:40

ready—prepared

> God's promises are,
> virtually, obligations that
> he imposes upon himself.
>
> *Friedrich Wilhelm Krummacher (1796-1868)*

The gospel will be preached to all nations before the Second Coming

This gospel of the kingdom will be *preached* in the whole world as a testimony to all nations, and then the *end* will come.

—MATTHEW 24:14

preached—proclaimed
end—culmination, goal, outcome

When Christ comes, we will receive resurrection bodies

Our citizenship is in heaven. And we eagerly await a Savior from there, the Lord Jesus Christ, who, by the *power* that enables him to bring everything under his *control*, will *transform* our lowly bodies so that they will be like his glorious body.

—PHILIPPIANS 3:20-21

power—energy
control—subjection, subordination
transform—change the form of, fashion anew

Christ will bring ultimate and final salvation when He returns

Christ was sacrificed once to take away the *sins* of many people; and he will appear a second time, not to bear sin, but to bring *salvation* to those who are waiting for him.

—HEBREWS 9:28

sins—wrongdoings, acts contrary to God's law
salvation—final rescue, ultimate deliverance

Christ will come in judgment at the Second Coming

Behold, I am coming soon! My *reward* is with me, and I will *give* to everyone according to what he has done.

—REVELATION 22:12

reward—what is paid back, wages
give—repay, render

Closeness to God

God will draw near to those who draw near to Him

Come near to God and he will come near to you.

—JAMES 4:8

The Lord is near to all who call on Him

The LORD is near to all who call on him, to all who call on him in *truth.*

—PSALM 145:18

truth—sincerity

We find God when we seek Him with all our heart

You will seek me and find me when you seek me with *all* your heart.

—JEREMIAH 29:13

all—the entirety of, the totality of

We are brought near to God through the blood of Jesus

In Christ Jesus you who once were *far away* have been brought near through the blood of Christ.

—EPHESIANS 2:13

far away—a long way off, distant

The pure in heart will see God

Blessed are the *pure* in heart, for they will see God.

—MATTHEW 5:8

blessed—happy, joyful, favored by God

pure—clean, innocent

Christ fellowships with the one who invites Him

Here I am! I stand at the door and knock. If anyone *hears* my voice and opens the door, I will come in and eat with him, and he with me.

—REVELATION 3:20

hears—pays attention to, understands, obeys

Comfort

The Lord is close to the brokenhearted

The LORD is close to the brokenhearted and saves those who are crushed in spirit.

—PSALM 34:18

God will wipe away every tear

The Lamb at the center of the throne will be their shepherd; he will lead them to springs of living water. And God will *wipe away* every tear from their eyes.

—REVELATION 7:17

wipe away—blot out, cancel, exterminate

The Lord will sustain us

Cast your *cares* on the LORD and he will *sustain* you; he will never let the righteous fall.

—PSALM 55:22

cast—throw, hurl

cares—burdens

sustain—uphold, support, bear up

Christ gives us rest

Come to me, all you who are *weary* and *burdened*, and I will give you *rest.*

—MATTHEW 11:28

weary—tired, labored
burdened—weighted down
rest—refreshment, relief

The Lord is our refuge

The LORD is *good*, a *refuge* in times of *trouble.* He cares for those who trust in him.

—NAHUM 1:7

good—desirable, morally good
refuge—stronghold, place of protection
trouble—distress, calamity

God comforts us

Praise be to the God and Father of our Lord Jesus Christ, the Father of *compassion* and the God of all *comfort*, who comforts us in all our *troubles*, so that we can *comfort* those in any trouble with the *comfort* we ourselves have received from God. For just as the sufferings of Christ flow over into our lives, so also through Christ our *comfort* overflows.

—2 CORINTHIANS 1:3-5

compassion—mercy, pity
comfort—consolation, encouragement
troubles—distresses, tribulations

Christ is always with us

Surely I am with you *always*, to the very end of the age.

—MATTHEW 28:20

always—perpetually, neverendingly, in all circumstances

God never promises more
than he is able to perform.

Anonymous

Companionship with God

Christ fellowships with those who invite Him

Here I am! I stand at the door and knock. If anyone *hears* my voice and opens the door, I will come in and eat with him, and he with me.

—REVELATION 3:20

hears—pays attention to, understands, obeys

The Lord is near to those who call on Him

The LORD is near to all who call on him, to all who call on him in *truth.*

—PSALM 145:18

truth—sincerity

We have fellowship with God when we walk in the light

If we *walk* in the light, as he is in the light, we have *fellowship* with one another, and the blood of Jesus, his Son, purifies us from all sin.

—1 JOHN 1:7

walk—conduct our lives

fellowship—intimate sharing

God draws near to those who draw near to Him

Come near to God and he will come near to you.

—JAMES 4:8

We find God when we seek Him with all our hearts

You will seek me and find me when you seek me with *all* your heart.

—JEREMIAH 29:13

all—the entirety of, the totality of

Compassion

The Lord is full of compassion

The Lord is full of *compassion* and *mercy*.

—JAMES 5:11

compassion—loving compassion, pity
mercy—tenderness

The Lord is compassionate to all

The LORD is *good* to all; he has *compassion* on all he has made.

—PSALM 145:9

good—pleasing, morally good
compassion—loving compassion, pity

God's compassion is like a loving parent's

As a father has *compassion* on his children, so the LORD has *compassion* on those who *fear* him.

—PSALM 103:13

compassion—loving compassion, pity
fear—worshipfully fear, show reverence to

The Lord's compassions never fail

Because of the LORD's great *love* we are not consumed, for his *compassions* never *fail.* They are *new* every morning.

—LAMENTATIONS 3:22-23

love—loyal love, faithful devotion
compassions—mercies
fail—cease, perish, deplete
new—refreshed

The Lord desires to show compassion

The LORD *longs* to be *gracious* to you; he rises to show you *compassion.* For the LORD is a God of justice. Blessed are all who wait for him!

—ISAIAH 30:18

longs—lies in wait, hopes for
gracious—charming, kind, merciful, compassionate
compassion—loving compassion, pity

Condemnation

There is no condemnation for those in Christ

There is *now* no *condemnation* for those who are in Christ Jesus.

—ROMANS 8:1

now—at the present time
condemnation—judging one guilty of wrongdoing

We are new creatures in Christ

If anyone is in Christ, he is *a new creation*; the old has *gone*, the *new* has come!

—2 CORINTHIANS 5:17

a new creation—altogether new
gone—passed away, come to an end, disappeared
new—fresh

God seeks to save us, not condemn us

God did not send his Son into the world to *condemn* the world, but to *save* the world through him. Whoever believes in him is not condemned, but whoever does not believe stands condemned already because he has not believed in the name of God's one and only Son.

—JOHN 3:17-18

condemn—pass judgment on

save—rescue, deliver, bring healing to

Trusting in Jesus rescues one from condemnation

Whoever *hears* my word and believes him who sent me has eternal life and will not be condemned; he has crossed over from death to life.

—JOHN 5:24

hears—understands, pays attention to, obeys

God has completely removed our transgressions

As far as the east is from the west, so far has he *removed* our *transgressions* from us.

—PSALM 103:12

removed—driven far away

transgressions—sins, rebellions

God will no longer remember our sins

I will forgive their *wickedness* and will remember their sins no more.

—HEBREWS 8:12

wickedness—wrongdoing, evil

God blots out our transgressions

I, even I, am he who *blots out* your transgressions, for my own sake, and remembers your sins no more.

—ISAIAH 43:25

blots out—exterminates, wipes out, washes off

Confession

C

God cleanses us of all sins when we confess

If we *confess* our sins, he is faithful and just and will *forgive* us our sins and purify us from all unrighteousness.

—1 JOHN 1:9

confess—admit, agree, acknowledge
forgive—pardon, remit, cancel

Confession to each other brings healing

Confess your *sins* to each other and pray for each other so that you may be healed. The prayer of a righteous man is powerful and effective.

—JAMES 5:16

confess—openly confess, admit freely
sins—wrongdoings, acts contrary to God's law

Our confession of Jesus brings salvation

If you *confess* with your mouth, "Jesus is Lord," and believe in your heart that God raised him from the dead, you will be *saved.*

—ROMANS 10:9

confess—declare, admit, acknowledge, agree
saved—rescued, delivered

Christ will acknowledge us if we acknowledge Him

Whoever *acknowledges* me *before* men, I will also acknowledge him before my Father in heaven.

—MATTHEW 10:32 (see also LUKE 12:8)

acknowledges—confesses, declares, admits
before—in the presence of, in front of

Confidence

We can do everything through Christ

I can do *everything* through him who gives me *strength.*

—PHILIPPIANS 4:13

everything—all things, anything
strength—inner empowerment

We are conquerors in Christ

In all these things we are *more than conquerors* through him who *loved* us.

—ROMANS 8:37

more than conquerors—complete in our conquest
loved—actively loved

Standing on the promises
of Christ my King,
Through eternal ages
let his praises ring;
Glory in the highest,
I will shout and sing,
Standing on the promises
of God.

R. Kelso Carter

We can be confident in approaching God

This is the *confidence* we have in approaching God: that if we ask anything according to his will, he hears us. And if we *know* that he hears us—whatever we ask—we *know* that we have what we asked of him.

—1 JOHN 5:14-15

confidence—bold assurance
know—know with certainty and assurance

C

Our confidence will be richly rewarded

Do not throw away your *confidence*; it will be richly rewarded. You need to *persevere* so that when you have done the will of God, you will receive what he has promised.

—HEBREWS 10:35-36

confidence—boldness, frankness
persevere—patiently endure

We should be unswerving, for God is faithful

Let us hold *unswervingly* to the *hope* we profess, for he who promised is faithful.

—HEBREWS 10:23

unswervingly—without wavering
hope—expectation

Conflict

Peacemakers are sons of God

Blessed are the *peacemakers*, for they will be called sons of God.

—MATTHEW 5:9

blessed—happy, joyful, favored by God
peacemakers—reconcilers

The God of peace is with us

Aim for perfection, listen to my appeal, be of one mind, live in peace. And the God of *love* and *peace* will be with you.

—2 CORINTHIANS 13:11

love—active love
peace—tranquility, serenity

Whatever you have learned or received or heard from me, or seen in me—put it into practice. And the God of *peace* will be with you.

—PHILIPPIANS 4:9

peace—tranquility, serenity

Christ gives us peace

Peace I leave with you; my *peace* I give you. I do not give to you as the world gives. Do not let your hearts be *troubled* and do not be *afraid.*

—JOHN 14:27

peace—tranquility, serenity
troubled—disturbed, terrified, thrown into confusion
afraid—timid, cowardly

Confusion

Christ's followers will not walk in darkness

I am the light of the world. Whoever follows me will never walk in darkness, but will have the light of life.

—JOHN 8:12

God gives us wisdom

If any of you *lacks* wisdom, he should ask God, who gives *generously* to all without finding fault, and it will be given to him.

—JAMES 1:5

lacks—is deficient in
generously—without reserve, liberally, ungrudgingly

God guides us

I will *instruct* you and *teach* you in the way you should go; I will *counsel* you and watch over you.

—PSALM 32:8

instruct—give understanding, give insight to, give wisdom to
teach—give guidance to
counsel—advise, give direction to

The Lord makes our steps firm

If the LORD *delights in* a man's way, he makes his steps *firm*; though he stumble, he will not fall, for the LORD *upholds* him with his hand.

—PSALM 37:23-24

delights in—is pleased with
firm—steadfast, established, secure
upholds—sustains, braces

God gives us a spirit of power

God did not give us a spirit of *timidity*, but a spirit of *power*, of love and of self-discipline.

—2 TIMOTHY 1:7

timidity—cowardice
power—ability

Consolation

The Lord is close to the brokenhearted

The righteous cry out, and the LORD hears them; he *delivers* them from all their *troubles*. The LORD is close to the brokenhearted and saves those who are crushed in spirit.

—PSALM 34:17-18

delivers—spares, saves, rescues
troubles—calamities, anguishes, distresses

The Lord heals the brokenhearted

He heals the brokenhearted and *binds up* their *wounds.*

—PSALM 147:3

binds up—bandages, wraps up
wounds—sorrows, griefs, pains

Christ gives us rest

Come to me, all you who are *weary* and *burdened,* and I will give you *rest.*

—MATTHEW 11:28

weary—tired, labored
burdened—weighted down
rest—refreshment, relief

The Lord sustains us

Cast your *cares* on the LORD and he will *sustain* you.

—PSALM 55:22

cast—throw, hurl
cares—burdens
sustain—hold up, support, bear up

The Lord is our refuge

The LORD is good, a *refuge* in times of *trouble.* He cares for those who trust in him.

—NAHUM 1:7

refuge—stronghold, place of protection
trouble—distress, calamity

Standing on the promises
that cannot fail,
When the howling storms
of doubt and fear assail,
By the living word of God
I shall prevail,
Standing on the
promises of God.

R. Kelso Carter

Contentment

The mind focused on God has perfect peace

You will *keep* in *perfect peace* him whose mind is steadfast, because he trusts in you.

—ISAIAH 26:3

keep—guard
perfect—complete and constant
peace—well-being, wholeness, tranquility

The mind controlled by the Spirit has peace

The mind of sinful man is death, but the mind controlled by the Spirit is life and *peace.*

—ROMANS 8:6

peace—tranquility, serenity

Turning our anxieties over to God yields perfect peace

Do not be *anxious* about anything, but in everything, by prayer and *petition,* with thanksgiving, present your requests to God. And the *peace* of God, which *transcends* all understanding, will *guard* your hearts and your minds in Christ Jesus.

—PHILIPPIANS 4:6-7

anxious—worried, concerned, fretful
petition—definite requests
peace—tranquility, serenity
transcends—surpasses, greatly exceeds
guard—shield

Be content, for God will provide

Do not *worry*, saying, "What shall we eat?" or "What shall we drink?" or "What shall we wear?" For the pagans run after all these things, and your heavenly Father knows that you need them. But *seek first* his kingdom and his righteousness, and all these things will be given to you as well.

—MATTHEW 6:31-33

worry—be concerned, have anxiety
seek—strive for, look for, desire
first—above all, earlier

Be content, for God will never forsake you

Keep your lives free from the love of money and be *content* with what you have, because God has said, "*Never* will I leave you; *never* will I forsake you."

—HEBREWS 13:5

content—satisfied
never—absolutely never

Be content, for God is in control

We know that in all things God works for the *good* of those who *love* him, who have been called according to his purpose.

—ROMANS 8:28

good—positive good, moral good
love—actively love

Courage

We can do all things through Christ

I can do *everything* through him who gives me *strength.*

—PHILIPPIANS 4:13

everything—all things, anything
strength—inner empowerment

God is completely for us

If God is for us, who can *be against* us? He who did not spare his own Son, but gave him up for us all—how will he not also, along with him, *graciously* give us all things?

—ROMANS 8:31-32

be against—successfully be against
graciously—freely

God upholds us

Do not fear, for I am with you; do not be dismayed, for I am your God. I will *strengthen* you and help you; I will *uphold* you with my righteous right hand.

—ISAIAH 41:10

strengthen—support, establish, harden against difficulties
uphold—take hold of, grasp firmly

D

Death

Those who follow Jesus never permanently die

I tell you the truth, if anyone *keeps* my word, he will never *see death.*

—JOHN 8:51

keeps—guards, obeys, observes
see—experience
death—permanent death

God will abolish death

He will *swallow up* death forever. The Sovereign LORD will *wipe away* the tears from all faces.

—ISAIAH 25:8

swallow up—consume, devour, gulp down
wipe away—blot out, exterminate

Death will be swallowed up in victory

When the perishable has been clothed with the imperishable, and the mortal with immortality, then the saying that is written will come true: "Death has been *swallowed up* in victory."

—1 CORINTHIANS 15:54

swallowed up—overwhelmed, drowned

Death cannot separate us from Christ

I am convinced that neither death nor life, neither angels nor demons, neither the present nor the future, nor any powers, neither height nor depth, nor anything else in all creation, will be able to *separate us* from the *love* of God that is in Christ Jesus our Lord.

—ROMANS 8:38-39

separate us—divide us, set us apart
love—active love

Permanent resurrection bodies await us

We know that if the earthly tent we live in is *destroyed*, we have a building from God, an eternal house in heaven, not built by human hands.

—2 CORINTHIANS 5:1

destroyed—thrown down, dissolved, abolished

God is our guide to the very end of our lives

This God is our God for ever and ever; he will be our guide even to the *end.*

—PSALM 48:14

D

end—death

> When thy secret hopes
> have perished
> In the grave of years gone by,
> Let this promise still be cherished,
> "I will guide thee with Mine eye."
>
> *Nathaniel Niles*

Decisions

God gives wisdom to those who ask in faith

If any of you *lacks* wisdom, he should ask God, who gives *generously* to all without finding fault, and it will be given to him.

—JAMES 1:5

lacks—is deficient in

generously—without reserve, liberally, ungrudgingly

God will guide us

I will *instruct* you and *teach* you in the way you should go; I will *counsel* you and watch over you.

—PSALM 32:8

instruct—give understanding to, give insight to, give wisdom to

teach—give guidance to

counsel—advise, give direction

The Holy Spirit will help and guide us

I will ask the Father, and he will give you another *Counselor* to be with you forever—the Spirit of truth.

—JOHN 14:16-17

Counselor—Intercessor, Helper, Advocate, One who encourages

Minds transformed by God and His Word can discern His will

Do not *conform* any longer to the pattern of this world, but be *transformed* by the renewing of your mind. Then you will be able to test and approve what God's will is—his good, pleasing and perfect will.

—ROMANS 12:2

conform—pattern after, fashion after, mold after

transformed—changed in form, molded

Dejection

God draws near to those who draw near to Him

Come near to God and he will come near to you.

—JAMES 4:8

Christ sympathizes with our weaknesses

We do not have a high priest who is unable to *sympathize* with our *weaknesses*, but we have one who has been tempted in every way, just as we are—yet was without sin.

—HEBREWS 4:15

sympathize—understand, have a shared feeling

weaknesses—infirmities

The Lord's compassions never fail

Because of the LORD's great *love* we are not consumed, for his *compassions* never *fail.* They are *new* every morning.

—LAMENTATIONS 3:22-23

love—loyal love, faithful devotion
compassions—mercies
fail—cease, perish, deplete
new—refreshed

God's love is everlasting

From everlasting to everlasting the LORD's *love* is with those who *fear* him.

—PSALM 103:17

love—loyal love, faithful devotion
fear—worshipfully fear, show reverence to

God provides absolute proof of His love

God *demonstrates* his own *love* for us in this: While we were still *sinners,* Christ died for us.

—ROMANS 5:8

demonstrates—proves
love—active love
sinners—complete moral failures

Deliverance

God guards Christians who fear Him

The angel of the LORD *encamps* around those who *fear* him, and he *delivers* them.

—PSALM 34:7

encamps—sets up camp around
fear—worshipfully fear, show reverence to
delivers—rescues, saves

The Lord delivers the righteous from trouble

The righteous cry out, and the LORD hears them; he *delivers* them from all their *troubles.*

—PSALM 34:17

delivers—rescues, saves
troubles—anguishes, calamities, distresses

The Lord rescues godly people

The Lord *knows how* to *rescue* godly men from trials.

—2 PETER 2:9

knows how—recognizes how, realizes how
rescue—deliver

God delivers us from our troubles

Call upon me in the day of trouble; I will *deliver* you, and you will honor me.

—PSALM 50:15

call upon—summon
deliver—rescue

The truth sets us free

You will *know* the truth, and the truth will *set you free.*

—JOHN 8:32

know—recognize, understand
set you free—liberate you, release you from bondage

Jesus sets us free

If the Son *sets you free,* you will be free *indeed.*

—JOHN 8:36

sets you free—liberates you, releases you from bondage
indeed—surely, certainly, truly

The Lord delivers us from Satan

The Lord is *faithful*, and he will strengthen and protect you from the evil one.

—2 THESSALONIANS 3:3

faithful—trustworthy, dependable, reliable

God delivers us from temptations

No *temptation* has *seized* you except what is common to man. And God is faithful; he will not let you be tempted beyond what you can *bear*. But when you are tempted, he will also provide a *way out* so that you can *stand up* under it.

—1 CORINTHIANS 10:13

temptation—trial, enticement to sin
seized—laid hold of, overtaken
bear—endure, resist
way out—means of escape
stand up—endure, bear up

Jesus helps us during temptations

Because he himself suffered when he was tempted, he is able to *help* those who are being tempted.

—HEBREWS 2:18

help—come to the aid of, assist, relieve

Depression

God heals the brokenhearted

He heals the brokenhearted and *binds up* their *wounds*.

—PSALM 147:3

binds up—bandages, wraps up
wounds—sorrows, griefs, pains

God comforts those who mourn

Blessed are those who *mourn*, for they will be *comforted.*

—MATTHEW 5:4

blessed—happy, joyful, favored by God

mourn—grieve

comforted—encouraged, exhorted

Turning our anxieties over to God yields perfect peace

Do not be *anxious* about anything, but in everything, by prayer and *petition*, with thanksgiving, present your requests to God. And the *peace* of God, which *transcends* all understanding, will *guard* your hearts and your minds in Christ Jesus.

—PHILIPPIANS 4:6-7

anxious—worried, concerned, fretful

petition—definite requests

peace—tranquility, serenity

transcends—surpasses, exceeds

guard—shield

God will deliver us from our troubles

Call upon me in the day of trouble; I will *deliver* you, and you will honor me.

—PSALM 50:15

call upon—summon

deliver—rescue

The Lord will sustain us in our troubles

Cast your *cares* on the LORD and he will *sustain* you.

—PSALM 55:22

cast—throw, hurl

cares—burdens

sustain—uphold, support, bear up

D

God empowers those who hope in Him

Those who *hope* in the LORD will *renew* their strength. They will *soar* on wings like eagles; they will run and not grow weary, they will walk and not be faint.

—ISAIAH 40:31

hope—wait for, look for
renew—replace, refresh
soar—be lifted up, be exalted

Suffering produces perseverance

We also *rejoice* in our *sufferings*, because we know that suffering produces *perseverance*.

—ROMANS 5:3

rejoice—boast, glory
sufferings—troubles, distresses, tribulations
perseverance—patient endurance

> If you would know experimentally the preciousness of the promises, and enjoy them in your own heart, meditate much upon them. There are promises which are like grapes in the wine-press; if you will tread them the juice will flow. Thinking over the hallowed words will often be the prelude to their fulfillment.
>
> *Charles Spurgeon*

Desertion

The Lord will never reject His people

The LORD will not *reject* his people; he will never *forsake* his inheritance.

—PSALM 94:14

reject—forsake, abandon, desert
forsake—desert, abandon

The Lord will never forsake us

Never will I leave you; *never* will I *forsake* you.

—HEBREWS 13:5

never—absolutely never
forsake—abandon, leave

The Lord will not forsake the faithful

The LORD *loves* the just and will not *forsake* his faithful ones. They will be *protected* forever, but the offspring of the wicked will be cut off.

—PSALM 37:28

loves—loves like a friend
forsake—desert, abandon
protected—guarded, watched over

Christ is with us always

Surely I am with you *always*, to the very end of the age.

—MATTHEW 28:20

always—perpetually, neverendingly, in all circumstances

Even when we are faithless, God remains faithful

If we are *faithless*, he will remain *faithful*, for he cannot *disown* himself.

—2 TIMOTHY 2:13

faithless—unfaithful, full of unbelief
faithful—trustworthy, reliable
disown—deny, renounce, repudiate

Despair

God gives us strength

He gives *strength* to the weary and *increases* the power of the weak.

—ISAIAH 40:29

strength—vigor, ability, power
increases—multiplies, enlarges

God is our refuge

God is our *refuge* and *strength*, an ever-present *help* in trouble.

—PSALM 46:1

refuge—shelter
strength—stronghold, fortification
help—support, ally

Christ provides relief

Come to me, all you who are *weary* and *burdened*, and I will give you *rest*.

—MATTHEW 11:28

weary—tired, labored
burdened—weighted down
rest—refreshment, relief

Our troubles fade in comparison to our future glory

We do not *lose heart*. Though outwardly we are *wasting away*, yet inwardly we are *being renewed* day by day. For our light and momentary *troubles* are achieving for us an eternal glory that far outweighs them all. So we *fix our eyes* not on what is seen, but on what is unseen. For what is seen is temporary, but what is unseen is eternal.

—2 CORINTHIANS 4:16-18

lose heart—give up, become discouraged, become wearied
wasting away—progressively decaying
being renewed—continuously renewed
troubles—distresses, tribulations
fix our eyes—look to, take notice of

Our perseverance in trials will yield the crown of life

Blessed is the man who *perseveres* under trial, because when he has stood the test, he will receive the crown of life that God has promised to those who love him.

—JAMES 1:12

perseveres—stands firm, endures

D

Determination

Christ is coming soon

I am coming *soon. Hold on* to what you have, so that no one will take your crown.

—REVELATION 3:11

soon—quickly, momentarily
hold on—seize, grab on

We will reap a harvest if we persevere

Let us not become *weary* in doing good, for at the proper time we will reap a harvest if we do not *give up*.

—GALATIANS 6:9

weary—discouraged, disheartened
give up—collapse in weariness

Confidence will be rewarded

Do not throw away your *confidence*; it will be richly rewarded. You need to *persevere* so that when you have done the will of God, you will receive what he has promised.

—HEBREWS 10:35-36

confidence—confident assurance, boldness, frankness
persevere—patiently endure

Devotion to God

The Lord strengthens those committed to Him

The eyes of the LORD *range* throughout the earth to *strengthen* those whose hearts are fully committed to him.

—2 CHRONICLES 16:9

range—roam about, wander
strengthen—encourage, empower, repair

The one who obeys will be blessed

The man who looks intently into the perfect law that gives *freedom,* and continues to do this, not forgetting what he has heard, but doing it—he will be *blessed* in what he does.

—James 1:25

freedom—liberty, freedom from enslavement
blessed—happy, joyful, favored by God

Christ answers the prayers of those devoted to Him

If you *remain* in me and my words *remain* in you, ask whatever you wish, and it will be given you.

—John 15:7

remain—abide, dwell, live

God's love made complete in those who obey

We know that we have come to know him if we *obey* his commands. The man who says, "I know him," but does not do what he commands is a liar, and the truth is not in him. But if anyone obeys his word, God's love is truly *made complete* in him.

—1 John 2:3-5

obey—observe, guard, keep
made complete—made perfect, fulfilled

> Standing on the promises
> of Christ the Lord,
> Bound to him eternally
> by love's strong cord,
> Overcoming daily
> with the Spirit's Sword,
> Standing on the
> promises of God.
>
> *R. Kelso Carter*

God loves those who obey

Whoever has my commands and *obeys* them, he is the one who *loves* me. He who *loves* me will be loved by my Father, and I too will love him and show myself to him.

—JOHN 14:21

obeys—observes, guards, keeps

loves—actively loves

Disappointment

God comforts those who mourn

Blessed are those who *mourn*, for they will be *comforted*.

—MATTHEW 5:4

blessed—happy, joyful, favored by God

mourn—grieve

comforted—encouraged, exhorted

The Lord is near to those who call on Him

The LORD is near to all who call on him, to all who call on him in *truth*.

—PSALM 145:18

truth—sincerity

Even in our troubles, God is working for our good

We know that in all things God works for the *good* of those who *love* him, who have been called according to his purpose.

—ROMANS 8:28

good—positive good, moral good

love—actively love

D

Discernment

God grants wisdom to those who ask in faith

If any of you *lacks* wisdom, he should ask God, who gives *generously* to all without finding fault, and it will be given to him.

—JAMES 1:5

lacks—is deficient in

generously—without reserve, liberally, ungrudgingly

Minds transformed by God and His Word can discern His will

Do not *conform* any longer to the pattern of this world, but be *transformed* by the renewing of your mind. Then you will be able to test and approve what God's will is—his good, pleasing and perfect will.

—ROMANS 12:2

conform—pattern after, fashion after, mold after

transformed—changed in form, molded

God will guide us

I will *instruct* you and *teach* you in the way you should go; I will *counsel* you and watch over you.

—PSALM 32:8

instruct—give understanding to, give insight to, give wisdom to

teach—give guidance to

counsel—give advice to, give direction to

Discipleship

True disciples are honored by God

Whoever *serves* me must follow me; and where I am, my servant also will be. My Father will *honor* the one who serves me.

—JOHN 12:26

serves—waits on, attends to

honor—show respect to, give recognition to

Whoever loses his life for Jesus will find it

If anyone would come after me, he must *deny* himself and take up his cross and follow me. For whoever wants to save his life will lose it, but whoever loses his life for me will find it.

—MATTHEW 16:24-25

deny—disown, repudiate, lose sight of, have no regard for

> He can hear the great petition,
> And the smallest, over there.
> Unto God pray without ceasing,
> He will answer every prayer.
>
> *Mary Bernstecher*

Disciples never walk in darkness

I am the light of the world. Whoever follows me will never walk in darkness, but will have the light of life.

—JOHN 8:12

Christ reveals Himself to obedient disciples

Whoever has my commands and *obeys* them, he is the one who *loves* me. He who loves me will be loved by my Father, and I too will love him and show myself to him.

—JOHN 14:21

obeys—observes, guards, keeps

loves—actively loves

We are Jesus' disciples when we obey

If you *hold to* my teaching, you are really my disciples.

—JOHN 8:31

hold to—remain in, stay in, dwell in, live in, obey

Disciples bear fruit when connected to Christ

Remain in me, and I will *remain* in you. No branch can bear fruit by itself; it must *remain* in the vine. Neither can you bear fruit unless you *remain* in me. I am the vine; you are the branches. If a man *remains* in me and I in him, he will bear much fruit; apart from me you can do *nothing.*

—JOHN 15:4-5

remain—abide, live, dwell
nothing—nothing at all, nothing in any way

Discipline

God disciplines those whom He loves

Those whom I love I *rebuke* and *discipline.* So be earnest, and *repent.*

—REVELATION 3:19

rebuke—show fault, expose, refute
discipline—train, instruct, educate
repent—change your mind, change your attitudes

God lovingly disciplines us as children

The Lord *disciplines* those he *loves,* and he *punishes* everyone he *accepts* as a son. *Endure* hardship as discipline.

—HEBREWS 12:6-7

disciplines—trains, instructs, educates
loves—actively loves
punishes—scourges, chastises
accepts—receives, welcomes
endure—patiently endure

God disciplines us for our good

God *disciplines* us for our good, that we may share in his holiness. No discipline seems pleasant at the time, but painful. Later on, however, it produces a harvest of righteousness and peace for those who have been trained by it.

—HEBREWS 12:10-11

disciplines—instructs, trains, educates

We are judged so we will not be condemned

When we are judged by the Lord, we are being *disciplined* so that we will not be condemned with the world.

—1 CORINTHIANS 11:32

disciplined—instructed, trained, educated

Scripture rebukes and corrects us

All Scripture is *God-breathed* and is useful for teaching, rebuking, correcting and training in righteousness.

—2 TIMOTHY 3:16

God-breathed—inspired

Discouragement

Perseverance will be rewarded

Do not throw away your *confidence*; it will be richly rewarded. You need to *persevere* so that when you have done the will of God, you will receive what he has promised.

—HEBREWS 10:35-36

confidence—confident assurance, boldness, frankness

persevere—patiently endure

We will reap a harvest if we don't give up

Let us not become *weary* in doing good, for at the proper time we will reap a harvest if we do not *give up.*

—GALATIANS 6:9

D

weary—discouraged, disheartened
give up—collapse in weariness

Christ gives us peace

Peace I leave with you; my *peace* I give you. I do not give to you as the world gives. Do not let your hearts be *troubled* and do not be *afraid.*

—JOHN 14:27

peace—tranquility, serenity
troubled—disturbed, terrified, thrown into confusion
afraid—timid, cowardly

The Lord renews the strength of those who hope in Him

Those who *hope* in the LORD will *renew* their strength. They will *soar* on wings like eagles; they will run and not grow weary, they will walk and not be faint.

—ISAIAH 40:31

hope—wait for, look for
renew—replace, refresh
soar—be lifted up, exalted

Disobedience

The one who obeys God is blessed

The man who looks intently into the perfect law that gives *freedom,* and continues to do this, not forgetting what he has heard, but doing it—he will be *blessed* in what he does.

—JAMES 1:25

freedom—liberty, freedom from enslavement
blessed—happy, joyful, favored by God

God's love is made complete in the one who obeys

If anyone *obeys* his word, God's love is truly made *complete* in him. This is how we *know* we are in him.

—1 JOHN 2:5

obeys—keeps, guards, observes
complete—perfect
know—recognize, understand

Obedience brings the blessing of fellowship with God

If anyone *loves* me, he will *obey* my teaching. My Father will love him, and we will come to him and make our *home* with him.

—JOHN 14:23

loves—actively loves
obey—keep, guard, observe
home—dwelling place, abode

People will be held accountable for disobedience

The Son of Man is going to come in his Father's glory with his angels, and then he will *reward* each person according to what he has done.

—MATTHEW 16:27

reward—pay back

Dissatisfaction

God is the true source of satisfaction

He *satisfies* the thirsty and fills the hungry with good things.

—PSALM 107:9

satisfies—satiates, fills and overfills

I will refresh the weary and satisfy the faint.

—JEREMIAH 31:25

Blessed are you who hunger now, for you will be satisfied.

—LUKE 6:21

Blessed—happy, joyful, favored by God

> From beginning to end, God is the giver and we are the receivers; and it is not to those who do great things, but to those who "receive abundance of grace, and of the gift of righteousness," that the richest promises are made.
>
> *Hannah Whitall Smith*

Those who seek the Lord find full satisfaction in Him

The lions may grow weak and hungry, but those who seek the LORD lack no good thing.

—PSALM 34:10

God brings satisfaction to those who delight in Him

Delight yourself in the LORD and he will give you the desires of your heart.

—PSALM 37:4

delight yourself—take your joy in

Divine Protection

God guards those who fear Him

The angel of the LORD *encamps* around those who *fear* him, and he *delivers* them.

—PSALM 34:7

encamps—sets up camp
fear—worshipfully fear, show reverence to
delivers—rescues

God protects the faithful

The LORD *loves* the just and will not *forsake* his faithful ones. They will be *protected* forever, but the offspring of the wicked will be cut off.

—PSALM 37:28

loves—loves like a friend
forsake—desert, abandon
protected—guarded, watched

God is our great protector

He will *cover* you with his feathers, and under his wings you will find refuge; his *faithfulness* will be your shield and rampart. You will not fear the terror of night, nor the arrow that flies by day, nor the pestilence that stalks in the darkness, nor the plague that destroys at midday.

—PSALM 91:4-6

cover—overshadow, conceal
faithfulness—trustworthiness, reliability

God rescues those who love Him

"Because he loves me," says the LORD, "I will *rescue* him; I will *protect him*, for he acknowledges my name."

—PSALM 91:14

rescue—deliver, bring to safety
protect him—keep him safe

God protects us from Satan

The Lord is *faithful*, and he will strengthen and protect you from the evil one.

—2 THESSALONIANS 3:3

faithful—trustworthy, dependable, reliable

Divine Provision

D

Have faith, for God will care for you

If that is how God clothes the grass of the field, which is here today, and tomorrow is thrown into the fire, how much more will he clothe you, O you of little faith!

—LUKE 12:28

God will meet all needs

My God will *meet* all your needs according to his glorious riches in Christ Jesus.

—PHILIPPIANS 4:19

meet—liberally fulfill, complete

God provides for those who fear Him

He provides food for those who *fear* him.

—PSALM 111:5

fear—worshipfully fear, show reverence to

Put God first, and temporal needs will be met

Seek first his kingdom and his righteousness, and all these things will be given to you as well.

—MATTHEW 6:33

seek—strive for, look for, desire

first—above all, earlier

God satisfies our hunger

He *satisfies* the thirsty and fills the hungry with good things.

—PSALM 107:9

satisfies—satiates, fills and overfills

Doubts of Salvation

God's people are sealed by the Holy Spirit

Having believed, you were *marked* in him with a *seal*, the promised Holy Spirit, who is a *deposit* guaranteeing our inheritance until the redemption of those who are God's possession.

—EPHESIANS 1:13-14

marked—stamped
seal—mark of possession, mark of identity
deposit—downpayment, pledge, foretaste

The Lord's arm is not too short to save

Surely the arm of the LORD is not too short to *save*, nor his ear too dull to hear.

—ISAIAH 59:1

save—rescue, deliver

Whoever believes in Jesus will be resurrected

I am the resurrection and the life. He who *believes in* me will live, even though he dies; and whoever lives and *believes in* me will never die.

—JOHN 11:25-26

believes in—trusts in, puts faith in, relies on

Those who believe are God's children

To all who received him, to those who *believed in* his name, he gave the *right* to become children of God.

—JOHN 1:12

believed in—put their trust in
right—authority, power

Salvation is a free gift rooted in God's grace

All have sinned and *fall short* of the glory of God, and are *justified freely* by his *grace* through the *redemption* that came by Christ Jesus.

—ROMANS 3:23-24

fall short—are in lack, are inferior, are destitute
justified—declared righteous
freely—without payment
grace—unmerited favor
redemption—ransom, release

Faith is credited as righteousness

To the man who does not *work* but trusts God who *justifies* the wicked, his faith is *credited* as righteousness.

—ROMANS 4:5

work—actively work, work to accomplish
justifies—declares righteous
credited—reckoned, counted, regarded

E

Elderly

Our bodies may age, but our spirits are renewed

We do not *lose heart.* Though outwardly we are *wasting away,* yet inwardly we are *being renewed* day by day.

—2 CORINTHIANS 4:16

lose heart—give up, become discouraged, become wearied
wasting away—progressively decaying
being renewed—continually renewed

The righteous bear fruit even in old age

The righteous will *flourish* like a palm tree, they will *grow* like a cedar of Lebanon; planted in the house of the LORD, they will *flourish* in the courts of our God. They will still bear fruit in old age, they will stay fresh and green.

—PSALM 92:12-14

flourish—blossom, sprout, bud
grow—be prosperous, increase

> Standing on the promises
> I cannot fall,
> List'ning ev'ry moment
> to the Spirit's call,
> Resting in my Savior
> as my all in all,
> Standing on the
> promises of God.
>
> *R. Kelso Carter*

God strengthens the weak

He gives *strength* to the weary and *increases* the power of the weak.

—ISAIAH 40:29

strength—vigor, ability, power
increases—multiplies, enlarges

God is our guide to the very end of our lives

This God is our God for ever and ever; he will be our guide even to the *end.*

—PSALM 48:14

end—death

Encouragement

God's mercies are new each morning

Because of the LORD's *great love* we are not consumed, for his *compassions* never fail. They are *new* every morning.

—LAMENTATIONS 3:22-23

great love—unfailing love, loyal devotion
compassions—mercies
new—fresh, renewed

God renews those who hope in Him

Those who *hope* in the LORD will *renew* their strength. They will *soar* on wings like eagles; they will run and not grow weary, they will walk and not be faint.

—ISAIAH 40:31

hope—wait for, look for
renew—replace, refresh
soar—be lifted up, exalted

The Lord sustains us in our troubles

Cast your *cares* on the LORD and he will *sustain* you.

—PSALM 55:22

cast—throw, hurl
cares—burdens
sustain—uphold, support, bear up

The Lord is good to those who hope in Him

The LORD is good to those whose hope is in him, to the one who seeks him; it is good to wait quietly for the *salvation* of the LORD.

—LAMENTATIONS 3:25-26

salvation—rescue, victory

Enemies

God guards those who fear Him

The angel of the LORD *encamps* around those who *fear* him, and he *delivers* them.

—PSALM 34:7

encamps—sets up camp
fear—worshipfully fear, show reverence to
delivers—rescues

God delivers the faithful

He *guards* the lives of his faithful ones and delivers them from the hand of the wicked.

—PSALM 97:10

guards—watches over, observes, keeps

God delivers the righteous

The righteous cry out, and the LORD hears them; he *delivers* them from all their *troubles.*

—PSALM 34:17

delivers—rescues, saves
troubles—anguishes, calamities, distresses

God delivers those who call on Him

Call upon me in the day of trouble; I will *deliver* you, and you will honor me.

—PSALM 50:15

call upon—summon
deliver—rescue

God is our powerful protector

He will *cover* you with his feathers, and under his wings you will find refuge; his *faithfulness* will be your shield and rampart. You will not fear the terror of night, nor the arrow that flies by day, nor the pestilence that stalks in the darkness, nor the plague that destroys at midday.

—PSALM 91:4-6

cover—overshadow, conceal

faithfulness—trustworthiness, reliability

Eternal Life

Those who believe in Jesus receive eternal life

For God so *loved* the world that he gave his one and only Son, that whoever *believes in* him shall not *perish* but have eternal life.

—JOHN 3:16 (see also JOHN 3:36)

loved—actively loved

believes in—trusts in, puts faith in, relies on

perish—come to destruction

Christians will be resurrected

I am the resurrection and the life. He who *believes in* me will live, even though he dies; and whoever lives and *believes in* me will never die.

—JOHN 11:25-26

believes in—trusts in, puts faith in, relies on

He who has the Son has life

This is the testimony: God has given us eternal life, and this life is in his Son. He who has the Son has life; he who does not have the Son of God does not have life.

—1 JOHN 5:11-12

Eternal life is a gift of God

The *wages* of sin is death, but the *gift* of God is eternal life in Christ Jesus our Lord.

—ROMANS 6:23

wages—compensation, payment
gift—gracious gift

The perishable will be made imperishable

The trumpet will sound, the dead will be raised *imperishable*, and we will be changed. For the perishable must clothe itself with the imperishable, and the mortal with immortality.

—1 CORINTHIANS 15:52-53

imperishable—immortal, lasting forever

> This old book [the Bible]
> is my guide;
> 'Tis a friend by my side.
> It will lighten and
> brighten my way.
> And each promise I find
> Soothes and gladdens my mind
> As I read it and
> heed it each day.
>
> *Edmund Pillifant*

Tears and death will pass away

He will *wipe* every tear from their eyes. There will be *no more* death or mourning or crying or pain, for the old order of things has passed away.

—REVELATION 21:4

wipe—blot out, exterminate
no more—absolutely no more

He will *swallow up* death forever. The Sovereign LORD will *wipe away* the tears from all faces.

—ISAIAH 25:8

swallow up—consume, devour, gulp down
wipe away—blot out, exterminate

Our eternal life is secure

My sheep *listen to* my voice; I know them, and they follow me. I give them eternal life, and they shall *never* perish; no one can *snatch* them out of my hand. My Father, who has given them to me, is greater than all; no one can *snatch* them out of my Father's hand.

—JOHN 10:27-29

listen to—understand, obey, pay attention to
never—never by any means
snatch—steal, carry off

Eternity

We will live with God face-to-face

Now the *dwelling* of God is with men, and he will *live* with them. They will be his people, and God himself will be with them and be their God. He will *wipe* every tear from their eyes. There will be no more death or *mourning* or crying or pain, for the old order of things has passed away.

—REVELATION 21:3-4

dwelling—abode, tent, tabernacle, shelter
live—encamp
wipe—blot out, exterminate, cancel
mourning—grief, sadness

Death will be swallowed up in victory

When the perishable has been clothed with the imperishable, and the mortal with immortality, then the saying that is written will come true: "Death has been *swallowed up* in victory."

—1 CORINTHIANS 15:54

swallowed up—overwhelmed, drowned

A wonderful destiny awaits those who love God

No eye has *seen*, no ear has heard, no mind has conceived what God has prepared for those who *love* him.

—1 CORINTHIANS 2:9

seen—perceived
love—actively love

Permanent resurrection bodies await us

We know that if the earthly tent we live in is *destroyed*, we have a building from God, an eternal house in heaven, not built by human hands.

—2 CORINTHIANS 5:1

destroyed—thrown down, dissolved, abolished

F

Failure

Your work is not in vain

Let nothing move you. Always give yourselves *fully* to the work of the Lord, because you know that your labor in the Lord is not *in vain.*

—1 CORINTHIANS 15:58

fully—in an abundant way, in an overflowing way
in vain—empty, empty-handed, useless, ineffective

Persevere, and you'll receive what God has promised

You need to *persevere* so that when you have done the will of God, you will *receive* what he has promised.

—HEBREWS 10:36

persevere—patiently endure
receive—be rewarded with

Stay confident, and you will be rewarded

Do not throw away your *confidence*; it will be richly rewarded. You need to *persevere* so that when you have done the will of God, you will receive what he has promised.

—HEBREWS 10:35-36

confidence—confident assurance, boldness, frankness
persevere—patiently endure

Faith

Faith in God can bring big results

Everything is possible for him who believes.

—MARK 9:23

I tell you the truth, if anyone says to this mountain, "Go, throw yourself into the sea," and does not *doubt* in his heart but believes that what he says will happen, it will be done for him.

—MARK 11:22-23

doubt—hesitate, waver

> Though troubles assail us
> and dangers affright,
> Though friends should all fail us and
> foes all unite,
> Yet one thing secures us,
> whatever betide,
> The promise assures us,
> "The Lord will provide."
>
> *John Newton*

Even small faith brings big results

I tell you the truth, if you have faith as small as a mustard seed, you can say to this mountain, "Move from here to there" and it will move. Nothing will be impossible for you.

—MATTHEW 17:20 (see also LUKE 17:6)

Those who have faith will do great things

I tell you the truth, anyone who has *faith* in me will do what I have been doing. He will do even greater things than these, because I am going to the Father.

—JOHN 14:12

faith—trust, belief

The prayer of faith can bring healing

Is any one of you *sick?* He should call the elders of the church to pray over him and *anoint* him with oil in the name of the Lord. And the prayer offered in faith will make the sick person *well;* the Lord will raise him up.

—JAMES 5:14-15

sick—ill, weak, ailing
anoint—pour out on
well—healed, delivered, rescued

Hearing God's Word increases our faith

Faith comes from hearing the message, and the message is heard through the word of Christ.

—ROMANS 10:17

F

Faithfulness

God and His promises are faithful

Let us hold *unswervingly* to the *hope* we profess, for he who promised is *faithful.*

—HEBREWS 10:23

unswervingly—without wavering
hope—expectation
faithful—trustworthy, reliable

God is faithful even when we are faithless

If we are *faithless,* he will remain *faithful,* for he cannot *disown* himself.

—2 TIMOTHY 2:13

faithless—unfaithful, full of unbelief
faithful—trustworthy, reliable
disown—deny, renounce, repudiate

The Lord faithfully protects us

The Lord is *faithful,* and he will strengthen and protect you from the evil one.

—2 THESSALONIANS 3:3

faithful—trustworthy, dependable, reliable

God is faithful in showing compassion

Because of the LORD's great *love* we are not consumed, for his *compassions* never *fail*. They are *new* every morning; great is your faithfulness.

—LAMENTATIONS 3:22-23

love—loyal love, faithful devotion
compassions—mercies
fail—cease, perish, deplete
new—refreshed

God is faithful through all generations

The LORD is good and his love endures forever; his faithfulness continues through all generations.

—PSALM 100:5

God will faithfully bring about what He has promised

What I have said, that will I bring about; what I have *planned*, that will I do.

—ISAIAH 46:11 (see also NUMBERS 23:19)

planned—sovereignly purposed

God is faithful to forgive us

If we *confess* our sins, he is *faithful* and *just* and will *forgive* us our sins and purify us from all unrighteousness.

—1 JOHN 1:9

confess—admit, agree, acknowledge
faithful—trustworthy, reliable
just—upright, righteous
forgive—pardon, remit, cancel

Fear

F

God has given us a spirit of power, not fear

God did not give us a spirit of *timidity*, but a spirit of *power*, of love and of self-discipline.

—2 TIMOTHY 1:7

timidity—cowardice
power—ability

We are sons of God, not slaves to fear

Those who are led by the Spirit of God are *sons* of God. For you did not receive a spirit that makes you a slave again to fear, but you received the Spirit of sonship. And by him we cry, "*Abba*, Father."

—ROMANS 8:14-15

sons—endeared children
Abba—dear daddy

God is our refuge

God is our *refuge* and *strength*, an ever-present *help* in trouble.

—PSALM 46:1

refuge—shelter
strength—stronghold, fortification
help—support, ally

God is our comforter, so we need not fear men

I, even I, am he who *comforts* you. Who are you that you fear mortal men, the sons of men, who are but grass?

—ISAIAH 51:12

comforts—consoles, expresses sympathy to

> Without the promise, prayer is eccentric and baseless. Without prayer, the promise is dim, voiceless, shadowy, and impersonal. The promise makes prayer dauntless and irresistible.
>
> *E.M. Bounds*

The Lord is our helper, so we need not be afraid

We say with confidence, "The Lord is my helper; I will not be *afraid.* What can man do to me?"

—HEBREWS 13:6

afraid—seized with alarm, fearful

God is our powerful protector

He will *cover* you with his feathers, and under his wings you will find refuge; his *faithfulness* will be your shield and rampart. You will not fear the terror of night, nor the arrow that flies by day, nor the pestilence that stalks in the darkness, nor the plague that destroys at midday.

—PSALM 91:4-6

cover—overshadow, conceal
faithfulness—trustworthiness, reliability

Fear of the Lord

The Lord delights in those who fear Him

The LORD *delights in* those who *fear* him, who put their hope in his *unfailing love.*

—PSALM 147:11

delights in—is pleased with
fear—worshipfully fear, show reverence to
unfailing love—loyal love and devotion

The Lord provides for those who fear Him

Fear the LORD, you his saints, for those who *fear* him lack nothing.

—PSALM 34:9

fear—worshipfully fear, show reverence to

The Lord's love is with those who fear Him

From everlasting to everlasting the LORD's *love* is with those who *fear* him, and his righteousness with their children's children.

—PSALM 103:17

love—loyal love and devotion

fear—worshipfully fear, show reverence to

The Lord has compassion on those who fear Him

As a father has *compassion* on his children, so the Lord has *compassion* on those who *fear* him.

—PSALM 103:13

compassion—mercy, pity

fear—worshipfully fear, show reverence to

The Lord fulfills the desires of those who fear Him

He fulfills the desires of those who *fear* him; he hears their cry and *saves* them.

—PSALM 145:19

fear—worshipfully fear, show reverence to

saves—rescues, delivers

The Lord watches over those who fear Him

The eyes of the LORD are on those who *fear* him, on those whose hope is in his *unfailing love.*

—PSALM 33:18

fear—worshipfully fear, show reverence to

unfailing love—loyal love and devotion

The Lord protects those who fear Him

The angel of the LORD *encamps* around those who *fear* him, and he *delivers* them.

—PSALM 34:7

encamps—sets up camp
fear—worshipfully fear, show reverence to
delivers—rescues

Fellowship

Christ fellowships upon invitation

Here I am! I stand at the door and knock. If anyone *hears* my voice and opens the door, I will come in and eat with him, and he with me.

—REVELATION 3:20

hears—pays attention, understands, obeys

The Lord is with those who gather in His name

If two of you on earth *agree* about *anything* you ask for, it will be done for you by my Father in heaven. For where two or three *come together* in my name, there am I with them.

—MATTHEW 18:19-20

agree—are in harmony
anything—anything and everything
come together—are gathered, are assembled

Those who love Jesus enjoy fellowship with God

If anyone *loves* me, he will *obey* my teaching. My Father will *love* him, and we will come to him and make our *home* with him.

—JOHN 14:23 (see also JOHN 14:21)

loves—actively loves
obey—keep, guard, observe
home—dwelling place, abode

We have fellowship with God if we walk in the light

If we claim to have *fellowship* with him yet *walk* in the darkness, we *lie* and do not live by the truth. But if we *walk* in the light, as he is in the light, we have *fellowship* with one another, and the blood of Jesus, his Son, purifies us from all sin.

—1 JOHN 1:6-7

fellowship—close association
walk—conduct our lives
lie—speak untruths

God lives in us if we love one another

No one has ever seen God; but if we *love* one another, God *lives in* us and his *love* is made complete in us.

—1 JOHN 4:12

love—actively love
lives in—abides with, remains in

Finances

Seek God's kingdom, and He will provide basic needs

Do not worry, saying, "What shall we eat?" or "What shall we drink?" or "What shall we wear?" For the pagans run after all these things, and your heavenly Father knows that you need them. But *seek first* his kingdom and his righteousness, and all these things will be given to you as well.

—MATTHEW 6:31-33

seek—strive for, look for, desire
first—above all, earlier

God will meet all our needs

My God will *meet* all your needs according to his glorious riches in Christ Jesus.

—PHILIPPIANS 4:19

meet—liberally fulfill, complete

Do not *worry* about your life, what you will eat; or about your body, what you will wear. Life is more than food, and the body more than clothes. Consider the ravens: They do not sow or reap, they have no storeroom or barn; yet God feeds them. And how much more valuable you are than birds!

—LUKE 12:22-24

worry—be concerned, have anxiety

God will never forsake you, so don't love money

Keep your lives free from the love of money and be content with what you have, because God has said, "*Never* will I leave you; *never* will I *forsake* you."

—HEBREWS 13:5

never—absolutely never
forsake—abandon, leave

> Prayer and the promises are interdependent. The promise inspires and energizes prayer.
>
> *E.M. Bounds*

Give, and it will be given to you

Give, and it will be given to you. A good measure, pressed down, shaken together and running over, will be poured into your lap. For with the measure you use, it will be measured to you.

—LUKE 6:38

If you sow sparingly, you will reap sparingly

Whoever sows sparingly will also reap sparingly, and whoever sows generously will also reap generously. God is able to make all grace abound to you, so that in all things at all times, having all that you need, you will *abound* in every good work.

—2 CORINTHIANS 9:6,8

abound—have more than enough, overflow

Food and Clothing

God will provide food and clothing

Do not *worry* about your life, what you will eat or drink; or about your body, what you will wear. Is not life more important than food, and the body more important than clothes? Look at the birds of the air; they do not sow or reap or store away in barns, and yet your heavenly Father feeds them. Are you not much more valuable than they?

—MATTHEW 6:25-26

worry—have anxiety, be concerned

God will provide clothing

If that is how God clothes the grass of the field, which is here today, and tomorrow is thrown into the fire, how much more will he clothe you, O you of little faith!

—LUKE 12:28

Seek God's kingdom, and He will meet basic needs

Do not worry, saying, "What shall we eat?" or "What shall we drink?" or "What shall we wear?" For the pagans run after all these things, and your heavenly Father knows that you need them. But *seek first* his kingdom and his righteousness, and all these things will be given to you as well.

—MATTHEW 6:31-33

seek—strive for, look for, desire

first—above all, earlier, first

God provides for those who fear Him

He provides food for those who *fear* him.

—Psalm 111:5

fear—worshipfully fear, show reverence to

God will meet all our needs

My God will *meet* all your needs according to his glorious riches in Christ Jesus.

—Philippians 4:19

meet—liberally fulfill, complete

Forgiveness

We are redeemed and forgiven

In him we have *redemption* through his blood, the *forgiveness* of sins, in accordance with the riches of God's *grace.*

—Ephesians 1:7

redemption—ransom, release from sin
forgiveness—pardon, cancellation of all debt
grace—unmerited favor

We are forgiven

He *forgave* us all our sins, having *canceled* the written code, with its regulations, that was against us and that stood opposed to us; he took it away, nailing it to the cross.

—Colossians 2:13-14

forgave—canceled the debt
canceled—blotted out, wiped away

God cleanses the stain of sin from our souls

"Come now, let us reason together," says the LORD. "Though your *sins* are like scarlet, they shall be as *white* as snow; though they are red as crimson, they shall be like wool."

—ISAIAH 1:18

sins—actions contrary to the law of God
white—whitened, spotless, purified

God completely removes our transgressions from us

As far as the east is from the west, so far has he *removed* our *transgressions* from us.

—PSALM 103:12

removed—driven far away
transgressions—sins, rebellions

God forgives our sins when we confess

If we *confess* our sins, he is faithful and just and will *forgive* us our sins and purify us from all unrighteousness.

—1 JOHN 1:9

confess—admit, agree, acknowledge
forgive—pardon, remit, cancel

God forgives our wickedness

I will forgive their *wickedness* and will remember their sins no more.

—HEBREWS 8:12

wickedness—wrongdoing, evil

God forgives us as we forgive others

If you forgive men when they *sin* against you, your heavenly Father will also forgive you. But if you do not forgive men their sins, your Father will not forgive your sins.

—MATTHEW 6:14-15 (see also LUKE 6:37)

sin—trespass, transgress, morally fail

> Nothing pleases our Lord better than to see His promises put in circulation; He loves to see His children bring them up to Him, and say, "Lord, do as Thou hast said." We glorify God when we plead His promises.
>
> *Charles Spurgeon*

Freedom

Christ sets us free

It is for *freedom* that Christ has set us free. *Stand firm*, then, and do not let yourselves be burdened again by a yoke of slavery.

—GALATIANS 5:1

freedom—liberty, freedom from bondage
stand firm—be steadfast, be immovable

If the Son *sets you free*, you will be free *indeed*.

—JOHN 8:36

sets you free—liberates you, frees you from bondage
indeed—surely, certainly, truly

The truth sets us free

You will *know* the truth, and the truth will *set you free.*

—JOHN 8:32

know—recognize, understand
set you free—liberate you, free you from bondage

Where the Spirit is, there is freedom

The Lord is the Spirit, and where the Spirit of the Lord is, there is *freedom.*

—2 CORINTHIANS 3:17

freedom—liberty, freedom from enslavement

Sin shall not be your master

Sin shall not be your *master*, because you are not under law, but under grace.

—ROMANS 6:14

master—lord, ruler, that which exercises authority

We are released from the law

By dying to what once *bound* us, we have been released from the law so that we serve in the new way of the Spirit, and not in the old way of the written code.

—ROMANS 7:6

bound—restrained, suppressed

Fresh Start

God's mercies are new every morning

Because of the LORD's great *love* we are not consumed, for his *compassions* never *fail.* They are *new* every morning.

—LAMENTATIONS 3:22-23

love—loyal love, faithful devotion
compassions—mercies
fail—cease, perish, deplete
new—refreshed

We are new creations in Christ

If anyone is in Christ, he is a *new creation*; the old has *gone*, the *new* has come!

—2 CORINTHIANS 5:17

new creation—altogether new
gone—passed away, come to an end, disappeared
new—fresh

Our spirits are renewed daily

We do not *lose heart.* Though outwardly we are *wasting away*, yet inwardly we are *being renewed* day by day.

—2 CORINTHIANS 4:16

lose heart—give up, become discouraged, become wearied
wasting away—progressively decaying
being renewed—continually renewed

Those who hope in the Lord receive renewed strength

Those who *hope* in the LORD will *renew* their strength. They will *soar* on wings like eagles; they will run and not grow weary, they will walk and not be faint.

—ISAIAH 40:31

hope—wait for, look for
renew—replace, refresh
soar—be lifted up, exalted

With renewed minds we can discern God's will

Do not *conform* any longer to the pattern of this world, but be *transformed* by the renewing of your mind. Then you will be able to test and approve what God's will is—his good, pleasing and perfect will.

—ROMANS 12:2

conform—pattern after, fashion after, mold after
transformed—changed in form, molded

Friendship of God

We are Christ's friends if we obey Him

You are my friends if you do what I *command.*

—JOHN 15:14

command—order, instruct

Obedience brings fellowship with God

If anyone *loves* me, he will *obey* my teaching. My Father will *love* him, and we will come to him and make our *home* with him.

—JOHN 14:23

loves—actively loves
obey—keep, guard, observe
home—dwelling place, abode

Christ fellowships upon invitation

Here I am! I stand at the door and knock. If anyone *hears* my voice and opens the door, I will come in and eat with him, and he with me.

—REVELATION 3:20

hears—pays attention, understands, obeys

The Lord is near to those who call on Him

The LORD is near to all who call on him, to all who call on him in *truth.*

—PSALM 145:18

truth—sincerity

God draws near to those who draw near to Him

Come near to God and he will come near to you.

—JAMES 4:8

Fruitfulness

The righteous bear fruit

The righteous will *flourish* like a palm tree, they will *grow* like a cedar of Lebanon; planted in the house of the LORD, they will *flourish* in the courts of our God. They will still bear fruit in old age, they will stay fresh and green.

—PSALM 92:12-14

flourish—blossom, sprout, bud
grow—be prosperous, increase

Those who trust in the Lord bear fruit

Blessed is the man who *trusts in* the LORD, whose *confidence* is in him. He will be like a tree planted by the water that sends out its roots by the stream. It does not fear when heat comes; its leaves are always green. It has no worries in a year of drought and never fails to bear fruit.

—JEREMIAH 17:7-8

trusts in—relies on, puts confidence in
confidence—security, firm trust

He who delights in God's Word bears fruit

Blessed is the man who does not walk in the counsel of the wicked or stand in the way of sinners or sit in the seat of mockers. But his *delight* is in the law of the LORD, and on his law he meditates day and night. He is like a tree planted by streams of water, which yields its fruit in season and whose leaf does not wither. Whatever he does *prospers.*

—PSALM 1:1-3

blessed—happy, joyful, favored by God
delight—pleasure, desire
prospers—succeeds, prevails

Those who abide in Christ bear fruit

I am the vine; you are the branches. If a man *remains* in me and I in him, he will bear much fruit; apart from me you can do *nothing.*

—JOHN 15:5

remains—lives, dwells, abides
nothing—nothing at all, nothing in any way

> God's promises cover all things which pertain to life and godliness, which relate to body and soul, which have to do with time and eternity. These promises bless the present and stretch out in their benefactions to the illimitable and eternal future.
>
> *E.M. Bounds*

Frustration

The Lord is our refuge

The LORD is good, a *refuge* in times of *trouble.* He cares for those who trust in him.

—NAHUM 1:7 (see also PSALM 34:17)

refuge—stronghold, place of protection
trouble—distress, calamity

The Lord will sustain us in our troubles

Cast your *cares* on the LORD and he will *sustain* you; he will never let the righteous fall.

—PSALM 55:22

cast—throw, hurl
cares—burdens
sustain—uphold, support, bear up

Even in our troubles, God is working for our good

We know that in all things God works for the *good* of those who *love* him, who have been called according to his purpose.

—ROMANS 8:28

good—positive good, moral good
love—actively love

Perseverance yields the crown of life

Blessed is the man who *perseveres* under trial, because when he has stood the test, he will receive the crown of life that God has promised to those who love him.

—JAMES 1:12

perseveres—stands firm, endures

The mind focused on God has perfect peace

You will keep in perfect *peace* him whose mind is steadfast, because he trusts in you.

—ISAIAH 26:3

peace—tranquility, wholeness, sense of well-being

A love for God's Word yields peace

Great *peace* have they who love your law, and nothing can make them stumble.

—PSALM 119:165

peace—tranquility, wholeness, sense of well-being

Fulfilled Life

Christ came to give us an abundant life

I have come that they may have life, and have it *to the full.*

—JOHN 10:10

to the full—abundantly, overflowing

God is the true source of satisfaction

He *satisfies* the thirsty and fills the hungry with good things.

—PSALM 107:9

satisfies—satiates, fills and overfills

Jesus satisfies spiritual hunger

Jesus declared, "I am the bread of life. He who comes to me will *never* go hungry, and he who *believes in* me will *never* be thirsty."

—JOHN 6:35

never—absolutely never

believes in—trusts in, puts faith in, relies on

Everyone who drinks this water will be thirsty again, but whoever drinks the water I give him will never thirst. Indeed, the water I give him will become in him a spring of water welling up to eternal life.

—JOHN 4:13-14

Future

A wonderful destiny awaits those who love God

No eye has *seen*, no ear has heard, no mind has conceived what God has prepared for those who *love* him.

—1 CORINTHIANS 2:9

seen—perceived
love—actively love

Our citizenship is in heaven

Our citizenship is in heaven. And we eagerly await a Savior from there, the Lord Jesus Christ, who, by the *power* that enables him to bring everything under his *control*, will *transform* our lowly bodies so that they will be like his glorious body.

—PHILIPPIANS 3:20-21

power—energy
control—subjection, subordination
transform—change the form of, fashion anew

Our perishable bodies will be made imperishable

The trumpet will sound, the dead will be raised *imperishable*, and we will be changed. For the perishable must clothe itself with the imperishable, and the mortal with immortality.

—1 CORINTHIANS 15:52-53

imperishable—immortal, lasting forever

We will live with Christ

In my Father's house are many rooms.... I am going there to prepare a place for you. And if I go and prepare a place for you, I will come back and take you to be with me that you also may be where I am.

—JOHN 14:2-3

We are destined for glory

Dear friends, now we are children of God, and what we will be has not yet been made known. But we know that when he appears, we shall be like him, for we shall see him as he is.

—1 JOHN 3:2

When Christ, who is your life, appears, then you also will *appear* with him in glory.

—COLOSSIANS 3:4

appear—be revealed, be made known, be displayed

G

Generosity and Giving

Good comes to the generous

Good will come to him who is generous and lends freely, who conducts his affairs with justice.

—PSALM 112:5

Give, and it will be given to you

Give, and it will be given to you. A good measure, pressed down, shaken together and running over, will be poured into your lap. For with the measure you use, it will be measured to you.

—LUKE 6:38

If you sow generously, you will reap generously

Whoever sows sparingly will also reap sparingly, and whoever sows generously will also reap generously.

—2 CORINTHIANS 9:6

> You are a welcome guest at the table of the promises. Scripture is a never-failing treasury filled with boundless stores of grace. It is the bank of heaven; you may draw from it as much as you please, without let or hindrance.
>
> *Charles Spurgeon*

God is our supplier

Now he who supplies seed to the sower and bread for food will also supply and increase your store of seed and will enlarge the harvest of your righteousness. You will be made rich in every way so that you can be generous on every occasion, and through us your generosity will result in thanksgiving to God.

—2 CORINTHIANS 9:10-11

Glory

Our sufferings pale in comparison to our future glory

I consider that our present *sufferings* are not worth comparing with the glory that will be revealed in us.

—ROMANS 8:18

sufferings—misfortunes

Our future glory outweighs all present troubles

Our *light* and momentary *troubles* are *achieving* for us an eternal glory that far outweighs them all. So we *fix our eyes* not on what is seen, but on what is unseen. For what is seen is temporary, but what is unseen is eternal.

—2 CORINTHIANS 4:17-18

light—not burdensome
troubles—distresses, tribulations
achieving—accomplishing, bringing about, producing
fix our eyes—continually focus on

We will appear with Christ in glory

When Christ, who is your life, appears, then you also will *appear* with him in glory.

—COLOSSIANS 3:4

appear—be revealed, be made known, be displayed

Our bodies will be gloriously transformed

Our citizenship is in heaven. And we eagerly await a Savior from there, the Lord Jesus Christ, who, by the *power* that enables him to bring everything under his *control*, will *transform* our lowly bodies so that they will be like his glorious body.

—PHILIPPIANS 3:20-21

power—energy
control—subjection, subordination
transform—change the form of, fashion anew

God has given you His promise
That He hears and answers prayer.
He will heed your supplication
If you cast on Him your care.

Mary Bernstecher

God's Word

Scripture is inspired and leads us into truth

All Scripture is *God-breathed* and is *useful* for teaching, rebuking, correcting and training in righteousness, so that the man of God may be *thoroughly equipped* for every good work.

—2 Timothy 3:16-17

God-breathed—inspired
useful—valuable, profitable
thoroughly equipped—capable of meeting all demands, proficient

Obedience to God's Word yields blessing

The man who looks intently into the perfect law that gives *freedom*, and continues to do this, not forgetting what he has heard, but doing it—he will be *blessed* in what he does.

—James 1:25

freedom—liberty, freedom from enslavement
blessed—happy, joyful, favored by God

Meditating on God's Word brings success

Do not let this Book of the Law *depart* from your mouth; *meditate* on it day and night, so that you may be careful to do everything written in it. Then you will be prosperous and successful.

—Joshua 1:8

depart—leave, be removed
meditate—mutter silently to yourself

Those who love God's Word have peace

Great *peace* have they who love your law, and nothing can make them stumble.

—PSALM 119:165

peace—tranquility, wholeness, sense of well-being

Good News (Gospel)

G

Those who believe in Jesus receive eternal life

For God so *loved* the world that he gave his one and only Son, that whoever *believes in* him shall not *perish* but have eternal life.

—JOHN 3:16

loved—actively loved

believes in—trusts in, puts faith in, relies on

perish—come to destruction

We are brought near to God through Christ

In Christ Jesus you who once were *far away* have been brought near through the blood of Christ.

—EPHESIANS 2:13

far away—a long way off, distant

Jesus took our sin and gave us His righteousness

God made him who had no *sin* to be sin for us, so that in him we might become the righteousness of God.

—2 CORINTHIANS 5:21

sin—wrongdoing, acts contrary to God's will

God loved us when we were still sinners

God *demonstrates* his own *love* for us in this: While we were still *sinners*, Christ died for us.

—ROMANS 5:8

demonstrates—proves
love—active love
sinners—complete moral failures

We are forgiven

He *forgave* us all our sins, having *canceled* the written code, with its regulations, that was against us and that stood opposed to us; he took it away, nailing it to the cross.

—COLOSSIANS 2:13-14

forgave—canceled the debt
canceled—blotted out, wiped away

Goodness

The Lord is good

The LORD is *good*, a *refuge* in times of *trouble*. He cares for those who trust in him.

—NAHUM 1:7

good—desirable, morally good
refuge—stronghold, place of protection
trouble—distress, calamity

The LORD is *good* and his *love* endures forever; his faithfulness continues through all generations.

—PSALM 100:5

good—desirable, pleasing, full of goodness
love—faithful love, loyal devotion

The Lord is good to all

The LORD is *good* to all; he has *compassion* on all he has made.

—PSALM 145:9

good—pleasing, desirable, morally good
compassion—mercy, pity

Even in our troubles, God is working for our good

We know that in all things God works for the *good* of those who *love* him, who have been called according to his purpose.

—ROMANS 8:28

good—positive good, moral good
love—actively love

God continues to do His good work in us

He who began a good *work* in you will carry it on to *completion* until the day of Christ Jesus.

—PHILIPPIANS 1:6

work—activity, task, deed, job
completion—perfection, the finish

God has prepared good works for us to do

We are God's *workmanship*, created in Christ Jesus to do good works, which God prepared in advance for us to do.

—EPHESIANS 2:10

workmanship—creation

Grace

We are saved by grace

Because of his great *love* for us, God, who is rich in mercy, made us alive with Christ even when we were dead in transgressions—it is by *grace* you have been saved.

—EPHESIANS 2:4-5

love—active love
grace—unmerited favor

It is by *grace* you have been saved, through faith—and this not from yourselves, it is the gift of God—*not* by works, so that no one can *boast.*

—EPHESIANS 2:8-9

grace—unmerited favor
not—not in any way, not at all
boast—brag

Our salvation demonstrates God's grace

God raised us up with Christ and seated us with him in the heavenly realms in Christ Jesus, in order that in the coming ages he might show the *incomparable riches* of his *grace,* expressed in his kindness to us in Christ Jesus.

—EPHESIANS 2:6-7

incomparable riches—limitless and immeasurable wealth
grace—unmerited favor

Christians enjoy a permanent standing in grace

Since we have been *justified* through faith, we have *peace* with God through our Lord Jesus Christ, through whom we have gained *access* by faith into this grace in which we now *stand.* And we rejoice in the hope of the glory of God.

—ROMANS 5:1-2

justified—declared righteous
peace—harmony, tranquility
access—free access, free approach
stand—stand firm, stand established

God gives you the grace you need to do good

God is able to make all *grace abound* to you, so that in all things at all times, having all that you need, you will *abound* in every good work.

—2 Corinthians 9:8

grace—unmerited favor, kindness

abound—overflow

The God of grace restores us

The God of all *grace*, who called you to his eternal glory in Christ, after you have suffered a little while, will himself *restore* you and make you strong, firm and steadfast.

—1 Peter 5:10

grace—unmerited favor

restore—mend, make complete

Grief

The death of Christians is precious to God

Precious in the sight of the Lord is the death of his *saints.*

—Psalm 116:15

precious—important, valuable

saints—holy ones, godly ones

Death is not the end

We do not want you to be ignorant about those who *fall asleep*, or to *grieve* like the rest of men, who have no hope....The dead in Christ will rise first. After that, we who are still alive and are left will be caught up together with them in the clouds to meet the Lord in the air. And so we will be with the Lord forever.

—1 Thessalonians 4:13-17

fall asleep—sleep in death

grieve—be sorrowful, distressed, sad, mournful

God comforts those who mourn

Blessed are those who *mourn*, for they will be *comforted.*

—MATTHEW 5:4

blessed—happy, joyful, favored by God
mourn—grieve
comforted—encouraged, exhorted

God will wipe away every tear in heaven

Now the *dwelling* of God is with men, and he will *live* with them. They will be his people, and God himself will be with them and be their God. He will *wipe* every tear from their eyes. There will be no more death or *mourning* or crying or pain, for the old order of things has passed away.

—REVELATION 21:3-4

dwelling—abode, tent, tabernacle, shelter
live—encamp
wipe—blot out, exterminate, cancel
mourning—grief, sadness

> Thy promises of grace
> Are pillars to support my hope,
> And there I write thy praise.
>
> *Isaac Watts*

God comforts us in our hurts

Praise be to the God and Father of our Lord Jesus Christ, the Father of *compassion* and the God of all *comfort,* who comforts us in all our *troubles,* so that we can comfort those in any trouble with the comfort we ourselves have received from God.

—2 CORINTHIANS 1:3-4

compassion—mercy, pity
comfort—consolation, encouragement
troubles—distresses, tribulations

Growth, Spiritual

God daily continues His work in us

He who began a good *work* in you will carry it on to *completion* until the day of Christ Jesus.

—PHILIPPIANS 1:6

work—activity, task, deed, job
completion—perfection, the finish

We are molded in Christ's image

We, who with unveiled faces all reflect the Lord's glory, are being *transformed* into his *likeness* with ever-increasing glory, which comes from the Lord, who is the Spirit.

—2 CORINTHIANS 3:18

transformed—changed in form, transfigured
likeness—image, portrait

Our renewed minds can discern God's will

Do not *conform* any longer to the pattern of this world, but be *transformed* by the renewing of your mind. Then you will be able to test and approve what God's will is—his good, pleasing and perfect will.

—ROMANS 12:2

conform—pattern after, fashion after, mold after
transformed—changed in form, molded

Guarded by God

The Lord protects those who fear Him

The angel of the LORD *encamps* around those who *fear* him, and he *delivers* them.

—PSALM 34:7

encamps—sets up camp
fear—worshipfully fear, show reverence to
delivers—rescues

God is our powerful protector

He will *cover* you with his feathers, and under his wings you will find refuge; his *faithfulness* will be your shield and rampart. You will not fear the terror of night, nor the arrow that flies by day, nor the pestilence that stalks in the darkness, nor the plague that destroys at midday.

—PSALM 91:4-6

cover—overshadow, conceal

faithfulness—trustworthiness, reliability

The Lord protects us from Satan

The Lord is *faithful*, and he will strengthen and protect you from the evil one.

—2 THESSALONIANS 3:3

faithful—trustworthy, dependable, reliable

Guidance

God will guide us

I will *instruct* you and *teach* you in the way you should go; I will *counsel* you and watch over you.

—PSALM 32:8

instruct—give understanding to, give insight to, give wisdom to

teach—give guidance to

counsel—advise, give direction to

God is our guide to the very end of our lives

This God is our God for ever and ever; he will be our guide even to the *end*.

—PSALM 48:14

end—death

The Holy Spirit will guide us

The *Counselor*, the Holy Spirit, whom the Father will send in my name, will teach you all things and will remind you of everything I have said to you.

—JOHN 14:26

Counselor—Intercessor, Helper, Advocate, One who encourages

The Lord guides those who delight in Him

If the LORD *delights in* a man's way, he makes his steps *firm*; though he stumble, he will not fall, for the LORD *upholds* him with his hand.

—PSALM 37:23-24

delights in—is pleased with
firm—steadfast, established, secure
upholds—sustains, braces

Our renewed minds can discern God's will

Do not *conform* any longer to the pattern of this world, but be *transformed* by the renewing of your mind. Then you will be able to test and approve what God's will is—his good, pleasing and perfect will.

—ROMANS 12:2

conform—pattern after, fashion after, mold after
transformed—changed in form, molded

Guilt

We are new creatures in Christ

If anyone is in Christ, he is a *new creation*; the old has *gone*, the *new* has come!

—2 CORINTHIANS 5:17

new creation—altogether new
gone—passed away, come to an end, disappeared
new—fresh

Those in Christ are not condemned

There is *now* no *condemnation* for those who are in Christ Jesus.

—ROMANS 8:1

now—at the present time

condemnation—judging one guilty of wrongdoing

We are forgiven

He *forgave* us all our sins, having *canceled* the written code, with its regulations, that was against us and that stood opposed to us; he took it away, nailing it to the cross.

—COLOSSIANS 2:13-14

forgave—canceled the debt

canceled—blotted out, wiped away

God blots out our transgressions

I, even I, am he who *blots out* your transgressions, for my own sake, and remembers your sins no more.

—ISAIAH 43:25

blots out—exterminates, wipes out, washes off

> God hath promised
> strength for the day,
> Rest for the labor, light for the way,
> Grace for the trials, help from above,
> Unfailing sympathy, undying love.
>
> *Annie J. Flint*

God completely removes our sins

As far as the east is from the west, so far has he *removed* our *transgressions* from us.

—PSALM 103:12

removed—driven far away

transgressions—sins, rebellions

God will no longer remember our sins

I will forgive their *wickedness* and will remember their sins no more.

—HEBREWS 8:12

wickedness—wrongdoing, evil

God forgives us when we confess

If we *confess* our sins, he is faithful and just and will *forgive* us our sins and purify us from all unrighteousness.

—1 JOHN 1:9

confess—admit, agree, acknowledge

forgive—pardon, remit, cancel

H

Happiness

A wonderful destiny awaits those who love God

No eye has *seen*, no ear has heard, no mind has conceived what God has prepared for those who *love* him.

—1 CORINTHIANS 2:9

seen—perceived

love—actively love

God will one day abolish tears and death

He will *wipe* every tear from their eyes. There will be *no more* death or mourning or crying or pain, for the old order of things has passed away.

—REVELATION 21:4

wipe—blot out

no more—absolutely no more

We can enjoy a perpetual Sabbath-rest

There remains, then, a Sabbath-rest for the people of God.

—HEBREWS 4:9

Healing

The prayer of faith can make a sick person well

Is any one of you *sick*? He should call the elders of the church to pray over him and *anoint* him with oil in the name of the Lord. And the prayer offered in faith will make the sick person *well;* the Lord will raise him up.

—JAMES 5:14-15

sick—ill, weak, ailing
anoint—pour out on
well—healed, delivered, rescued

Though outwardly wasting away, we are inwardly renewed

We do not *lose heart.* Though outwardly we are *wasting away*, yet inwardly we are *being renewed* day by day.

—2 CORINTHIANS 4:16

lose heart—give up, become discouraged, become wearied
wasting away—progressively decaying
being renewed—continually renewed

Permanent resurrection bodies await us

We know that if the earthly tent we live in is *destroyed*, we have a building from God, an eternal house in heaven, not built by human hands.

—2 CORINTHIANS 5:1

destroyed—thrown down, dissolved, abolished

Heaven

A wonderful destiny awaits those who love God

No eye has *seen*, no ear has heard, no mind has conceived what God has prepared for those who *love* him.

—1 CORINTHIANS 2:9

seen—perceived
love—actively love

God will one day abolish tears and death

He will *wipe* every tear from their eyes. There will be *no more* death or mourning or crying or pain, for the old order of things has passed away.

—REVELATION 21:4

wipe—blot out
no more—absolutely no more

Heaven has plenty of room

In my Father's house are many rooms.... I am going there to prepare a place for you. And if I go and prepare a place for you, I will come back and take you to be with me that you also may be where I am.

—JOHN 14:2-3

All needs will be met in heaven

Never again will they hunger; *never again* will they thirst. The sun will not beat upon them, nor any scorching heat. For the Lamb at the center of the throne will be their shepherd; he will lead them to springs of living water. And God will *wipe away* every tear from their eyes.

—REVELATION 7:16-17

never again—not in the slightest degree
wipe away—blot out, exterminate

Nothing impure will enter heaven

Nothing *impure* will ever enter it, nor will anyone who does what is *shameful* or deceitful, but only those whose names are written in the Lamb's book of life.

—REVELATION 21:27

impure—unholy, unclean
shameful—detestable, abominable

We will have glorious resurrection bodies in heaven

We know that if the earthly tent we live in is *destroyed*, we have a building from God, an eternal house in heaven, not built by human hands.

—2 CORINTHIANS 5:1

destroyed—thrown down, dissolved, abolished

> He will keep his promise to me,
> All the way with me He will go;
> He has never broken any
> promise spoken;
> He will keep His promise, I know.
>
> *James Rowe*

Help

The Lord's arm is not too short to save

Surely the arm of the LORD is not too short to *save*, nor his ear too dull to hear.

—ISAIAH 59:1

save—rescue, deliver

The Lord is a stronghold in times of trouble

The LORD is a refuge for the oppressed, a stronghold in times of trouble.

—PSALM 9:9 (see also NAHUM 1:7)

Christ helps us in our temptations

Because he himself suffered when he was tempted, he is able to *help* those who are being tempted.

—HEBREWS 2:18

help—come to the aid of, assist, relieve

God delivers those who cry out to Him

He will *deliver* the needy who cry out, the *afflicted* who have no one to help.

—PSALM 72:12

deliver—rescue, save
afflicted—oppressed

The Lord delivers the righteous from troubles

A righteous man may have many troubles, but the LORD delivers him from them all.

—PSALM 34:19

Disaster will not befall us

No harm will befall you, no disaster will come near your tent. For he will command his angels concerning you to *guard* you in all your ways.

—PSALM 91:10-11

guard—keep watch, observe

Precious promise God has given
To the weary passerby,
On the way from earth to heaven,
"I will guide thee with Mine eye."

Nathaniel Niles

Holy Spirit

God will pour out His Spirit in the last days

In the last days, God says, I will pour out my Spirit on all people. Your sons and daughters will prophesy, your young men will see visions, your old men will dream dreams.

—ACTS 2:17

The Holy Spirit indwells us

Whoever *believes in* me, as the Scripture has said, streams of living water will flow from within him. By this he meant the Spirit, whom those who believed in him were later to receive. Up to that time the Spirit had not been given, since Jesus had not yet been glorified.

—JOHN 7:38-39

believes in—trusts in, puts faith in

Living in dependence on the Spirit brings victory

Live by the Spirit, and you will not *gratify* the desires of the sinful nature.

—GALATIANS 5:16

live by—habitually walk in dependence on

gratify—fulfill

The Holy Spirit helps us by praying for us

The Spirit himself *intercedes* for us with groans that words cannot express.

—ROMANS 8:26

intercedes—pleads, prays

The Holy Spirit reminds us of the teachings of Jesus

The *Counselor*, the Holy Spirit, whom the Father will send in my name, will teach you all things and will remind you of everything I have said to you.

—JOHN 14:26

Counselor—Intercessor, Helper, Advocate, One who encourages

The Holy Spirit guides us

When he, the Spirit of truth, comes, he will *guide* you into all truth.

—JOHN 16:13

guide—lead, explain, instruct

Home with the Lord

We will live with God face-to-face

Now the *dwelling* of God is with men, and he will *live* with them. They will be his people, and God himself will be with them and be their God.

—REVELATION 21:3

dwelling—abode, tent, tabernacle, shelter

live—encamp

We will live forever in the place Jesus has prepared for us

In my Father's house are many rooms; if it were not so, I would have told you. I am going there to prepare a place for you. And if I go and prepare a place for you, I will come back and take you to be with me that you also may be where I am.

—JOHN 14:2-3

We will dwell in a new heaven and a new earth

Then I saw a new heaven and a new earth, for the first heaven and the first earth had *passed away*, and there was no longer any sea. I saw the Holy City, the new Jerusalem, coming down out of heaven from God, prepared as a bride beautifully *dressed* for her husband.

—REVELATION 21:1-2

passed away—vanished
dressed—adorned

In keeping with his promise we are *looking forward* to a new heaven and a new earth, the home of righteousness.

—2 PETER 3:13

looking forward—expectantly waiting for

Hope

We have a living hope

Praise be to the God and Father of our Lord Jesus Christ! In his *great mercy* he has given us new birth into a living *hope* through the resurrection of Jesus Christ from the dead.

—1 PETER 1:3

great mercy—superabundant compassion
hope—expectation

The hope of salvation is our helmet

Since we belong to the day, let us be *self-controlled*, putting on faith and love as a breastplate, and the hope of salvation as a helmet. For God did not appoint us to suffer wrath but to receive salvation through our Lord Jesus Christ.

—1 THESSALONIANS 5:8-9

self-controlled—clear-headed, sober-minded

God delivers those whose hope is in His unfailing love

The eyes of the LORD are on those who *fear* him, on those whose hope is in his *unfailing love.*

—PSALM 33:18

fear—worshipfully fear, show reverence to
unfailing love—loyal love and devotion

Those who hope in the Lord renew their strength

Those who *hope* in the LORD will *renew* their strength. They will *soar* on wings like eagles; they will run and not grow weary, they will walk and not be faint.

—ISAIAH 40:31

hope—wait for, look for
renew—replace, refresh
soar—be lifted up, exalted

> Believe the promises more firmly than you have done. Let faith increase in fullness, constancy, simplicity.
>
> *Charles Spurgeon*

Hospitality

Doing good to others is doing good to Christ

I tell you the truth, whatever you did for one of the *least* of these brothers of mine, you did for me.

—MATTHEW 25:40

least—most trivial, least significant

Charitable kindness to children brings blessing

If anyone gives even a cup of cold water to one of these little ones because he is my disciple, I tell you the truth, he will *certainly not* lose his *reward.*

—MATTHEW 10:42

certainly not—absolutely not
reward—what is paid back

Showing hospitality to enemies brings a reward

Love your enemies, do good to them, and lend to them without expecting to get anything back. Then your *reward* will be great, and you will be sons of the Most High, because he is kind to the ungrateful and wicked.

—LUKE 6:35

reward—wage, payback

Giving in secret brings a reward

When you *give* to the needy, do not let your left hand know what your right hand is doing, so that your giving may be in *secret.* Then your Father, who sees what is done in *secret,* will reward you.

—MATTHEW 6:3-4

give—charitably give
secret—hidden, unseen, undisclosed

Humility

The humble will be exalted

Whoever exalts himself will be humbled, and whoever humbles himself will be *exalted.*

—MATTHEW 23:12

exalted—lifted up, elevated

The humble will be lifted up

Humble yourselves before the Lord, and he will *lift you up.*

—JAMES 4:10

lift you up—exalt you, elevate you

Humble yourselves, therefore, under God's mighty hand, that he may *lift you up* in due time.

—1 PETER 5:6

lift you up—exalt you, elevate you

The Lord sustains the humble

The LORD sustains the humble but casts the wicked to the ground.

—PSALM 147:6

Becoming humble like a child yields greatness

I tell you the truth, unless you change and become like little children, you will never enter the kingdom of heaven. Therefore, whoever humbles himself like this child is the greatest in the kingdom of heaven.

—MATTHEW 18:3-4

The humble are crowned with salvation

The LORD *takes delight in* his people; he *crowns* the humble with salvation.

—PSALM 149:4

takes delight in—is pleased with
crowns—adorns, endows, honors

The Lord guides the humble

He guides the humble in what is right and teaches them his way.

—PSALM 25:9

I

Illness

The prayer of faith will make a sick person well

Is any one of you *sick*? He should call the elders of the church to pray over him and *anoint* him with oil in the name of the Lord. And the prayer offered in faith will make the sick person *well*; the Lord will raise him up.

—James 5:14-15

sick—ill, weak, ailing

anoint—pour out on

well—healed, delivered, rescued

Though outwardly wasting away, we are inwardly renewed

We do not *lose heart*. Though outwardly we are *wasting away*, yet inwardly we are *being renewed* day by day.

—2 Corinthians 4:16

lose heart—give up, become discouraged, become wearied

wasting away—progressively decaying

being renewed—continually renewed

God is our guide to the very end of our lives

This God is our God for ever and ever; he will be our guide even to the *end*.

—Psalm 48:14

end—death

Permanent resurrection bodies await us

We know that if the earthly tent we live in is *destroyed*, we have a building from God, an eternal house in heaven, not built by human hands.

—2 CORINTHIANS 5:1

destroyed—thrown down, dissolved, abolished

Inheritance

We are heirs of God and co-heirs with Christ

The Spirit himself *testifies* with our spirit that we are God's children. Now if we are children, then we are heirs—heirs of God and co-heirs with Christ, if indeed we share in his sufferings in order that we may also share in his glory.

—ROMANS 8:16-17

testifies—confirms

We are heirs according to the promise

If you belong to Christ, then you are Abraham's seed, and heirs according to the promise.

—GALATIANS 3:29

Our inheritance can never perish, spoil, or fade

In his great mercy he has given us new birth into a living hope through the resurrection of Jesus Christ from the dead, and into an inheritance that can never *perish*, spoil or fade—*kept* in heaven for you.

—1 PETER 1:3-4

perish—fade away, pass away

kept—guarded

We will receive an inheritance as a reward

Whatever you do, work at it with all your heart, as working for the Lord, not for men, since you know that you will receive an inheritance from the Lord as a reward. It is the Lord Christ you are *serving*.

—COLOSSIANS 3:23-24

serving—serving as a slave

The Holy Spirit is a deposit guaranteeing our inheritance

Having believed, you were marked in him with a *seal*, the promised Holy Spirit, who is a *deposit* guaranteeing our inheritance until the redemption of those who are God's possession—to the praise of his glory.

—EPHESIANS 1:13-14

seal—symbol of ownership, authority, identity
deposit—down payment, pledge

> The promises of God are "exceeding great and precious," words which clearly indicate their great value and their broad reach, as grounds upon which to base our expectations in praying.
>
> *E.M. Bounds*

Integrity

God withholds nothing from those whose walk is blameless

The LORD God is a sun and shield; the LORD bestows favor and honor; no good thing does he withhold from those whose walk is *blameless*.

—PSALM 84:11

blameless—unblemished, without defect

Those who yearn for righteousness will be filled

Blessed are those who hunger and thirst for righteousness, for they will be *filled.*

—MATTHEW 5:6

blessed—happy, joyful, favored by God
filled—filled to satisfaction, filled to the full

The fruit of righteousness is peace

The fruit of righteousness will be *peace;* the effect of righteousness will be quietness and *confidence* forever.

—ISAIAH 32:17

peace—well-being, contentment
confidence—security, safety

The upright enter peace

Those who walk *uprightly* enter into *peace.*

—ISAIAH 57:2

uprightly—honestly, properly, on the straight path
peace—wholeness, well-being, safety

J

Jesus

Whoever follows Jesus will never walk in darkness

I am the light of the world. Whoever follows me will never walk in darkness, but will have the light of life.

—JOHN 8:12

We have peace with God through Jesus

Since we have been *justified* through faith, we have *peace* with God through our Lord Jesus Christ.

—ROMANS 5:1

justified—declared righteous
peace—harmony, tranquility

Those in Christ are not condemned

There is *now* no *condemnation* for those who are in Christ Jesus.

—ROMANS 8:1

now—at the present time
condemnation—judging one guilty of wrongdoing

In Jesus we have redemption and forgiveness

In him we have *redemption* through his blood, the *forgiveness* of sins, in accordance with the riches of God's *grace.*

—EPHESIANS 1:7 (see also 1 PETER 1:18-19)

redemption—ransom, release from sin
forgiveness—pardon, cancellation of all debt
grace—unmerited favor, kindness

We become God's children through faith in Jesus

You are all *sons* of God through *faith* in Christ Jesus.

—GALATIANS 3:26

sons—endeared children
faith—belief, trust

God meets our needs according to His riches in Christ Jesus

My God will *meet* all your needs according to his glorious riches in Christ Jesus.

—PHILIPPIANS 4:19

meet—liberally fulfill, complete

If we acknowledge Jesus, He acknowledges us

Whoever *acknowledges* me before men, the Son of Man will also acknowledge him before the angels of God. But he who *disowns* me before men will be disowned before the angels of God.

—LUKE 12:8-9

acknowledges—admits, confesses, declares
disowns—renounces, repudiates, denies

Joy

Our names are written in heaven

Do not rejoice that the spirits submit to you, but rejoice that your names are written in heaven.

—LUKE 10:20

Those who sow in tears will reap joy

Those who sow in tears will reap with songs of joy. He who goes out weeping, carrying seed to sow, will return with songs of joy, carrying sheaves with him.

—PSALM 126:5-6

Obey Christ, and you will experience joy

If you *obey* my commands, you will *remain* in my love, just as I have obeyed my Father's commands and remain in his love. I have told you this so that my *joy* may be in you and that your *joy* may be complete.

—JOHN 15:10-11

obey—keep, guard, observe
remain—stay, live, dwell, abide
joy—rejoicing, happiness, gladness

Ask in Jesus' name, and your joy will be complete

Until now you have not asked for anything in my name. Ask and you will receive, and your *joy* will be *complete.*

—JOHN 16:24

joy—happiness, rejoicing, gladness
complete—fulfilled

Justice

All God's ways are just

He is the Rock, his works are *perfect,* and all his ways are just. A faithful God who does no wrong, *upright* and just is he.

—DEUTERONOMY 32:4

perfect—without defect, blameless
upright—righteous, innocent

The works of God's hands are just

The works of his hands are *faithful* and just; all his precepts are trustworthy.

—PSALM 111:7

faithful—trustworthy, reliable

The Lord is a God of justice

The LORD *longs* to be *gracious* to you; he rises to show you *compassion.* For the LORD is a God of justice. Blessed are all who wait for him!

—ISAIAH 30:18

longs—lies in wait, hopes for
gracious—charming, kind, merciful, compassionate
compassion—mercy, pity

The Lord loves the just

The LORD *loves* the just and will not *forsake* his faithful ones. They will be *protected* forever, but the offspring of the wicked will be cut off.

—PSALM 37:28

loves—loves like a friend
forsake—desert, abandon
protected—guarded, watched

Good comes to him who conducts his affairs with justice

Good will come to him who is generous and lends freely, who conducts his affairs with justice.

—PSALM 112:5

The Lord brings justice for the oppressed

The LORD works righteousness and justice for all the *oppressed.*

—PSALM 103:6

oppressed—mistreated

> With this hope therefore let our souls be bound unto Him that is faithful in His promises and that is righteous in His judgments.
>
> *1 Clement 27:1*

Justification

We are justified in the name of Jesus

You were washed, you were *sanctified*, you were *justified* in the name of the Lord Jesus Christ and by the Spirit of our God.

—1 CORINTHIANS 6:11

sanctified—set apart
justified—declared righteous

Jesus took our sin and gave us His righteousness

God made him who had no *sin* to be *sin* for us, so that in him we might become the righteousness of God.

—2 CORINTHIANS 5:21

sin—wrongdoing, acts contrary to God's will

Jesus was raised to life for our justification

He was *delivered over* to death for our sins and was raised to life for our *justification*.

—ROMANS 4:25

delivered over—betrayed, handed over
justification—declaration of righteousness

We are justified through faith

When a man works, his *wages* are not *credited* to him as a *gift*, but as an *obligation*. However, to the man who does not work but trusts God who *justifies* the wicked, his faith is credited as righteousness.

—ROMANS 4:4-5

wages—reward, what is paid back
credited—reckoned, counted
gift—grace gift
obligation—debt
justifies—declares righteous

Since we have been *justified* through faith, we have *peace* with God through our Lord Jesus Christ.

—ROMANS 5:1

justified—declared righteous
peace—harmony, tranquility

Because we are justified, we are saved from God's wrath

Since we have now been *justified* by his blood, how much more shall we be *saved* from God's *wrath* through him!

—ROMANS 5:9

justified—declared righteous
saved—rescued, delivered
wrath—anger, displeasure, hostility

K

Kindness of God

The Lord has compassion on all

The LORD is good to all; he has *compassion* on all he has made.

—PSALM 145:9

compassion—mercy, pity

The Lord has compassion on those who fear Him

As a father has *compassion* on his children, so the LORD has *compassion* on those who fear him.

—PSALM 103:13

compassion—mercy, pity

God's mercies are new every morning

Because of the LORD's great *love* we are not consumed, for his *compassions* never *fail.* They are *new* every morning.

—LAMENTATIONS 3:22-23

love—loyal love, faithful devotion
compassions—mercies
fail—cease, perish, deplete
new—refreshed

We are saved because of God's kindness and mercy

When the kindness and love of God our Savior appeared, he *saved* us, not because of righteous things we had done, but because of his *mercy.* He saved us through the washing of *rebirth* and renewal by the Holy Spirit.

—TITUS 3:4-5

saved—rescued, delivered
mercy—compassion, pity, kindness
rebirth—regeneration

God's kindness is expressed in Jesus

God raised us up with Christ and seated us with him in the heavenly realms in Christ Jesus, in order that in the coming ages he might show the *incomparable riches* of his *grace,* expressed in his kindness to us in Christ Jesus.

—EPHESIANS 2:6-7

incomparable riches—limitless wealth, immeasurable wealth
grace—unmerited favor

Kingdom of God

God's kingdom rules over all

The LORD has *established* his throne in heaven, and his kingdom *rules* over all.

—PSALM 103:19

established—set in place, prepared
rules—governs, has dominion

God has brought us into His kingdom

He has rescued us from the *dominion* of darkness and brought us into the *kingdom* of the Son he loves, in whom we have redemption, the forgiveness of sins.

—COLOSSIANS 1:13-14

dominion—authority, power, right to control
kingdom—royal rule

Seek God's kingdom first, and He will meet your needs

Seek first his kingdom and his righteousness, and all these things will be given to you as well.

—MATTHEW 6:33

seek—strive for, look for, desire
first—above all, earlier

Obedience leads to greatness in the kingdom

Anyone who *breaks* one of the *least* of these commandments and teaches others to do the same will be called *least* in the kingdom of heaven, but whoever practices and teaches these commands will be called great in the kingdom of heaven.

—MATTHEW 5:19

breaks—does away with, relaxes
least—most trivial

Humility leads to greatness in the kingdom

Whoever *humbles himself* like this child is the greatest in the kingdom of heaven.

—MATTHEW 18:4

humbles himself—lowers himself

L

Liberty

Obedience to God's Word brings freedom

The man who looks intently into the perfect law that gives *freedom*, and continues to do this, not forgetting what he has heard, but doing it—he will be *blessed* in what he does.

—JAMES 1:25

freedom—liberty, freedom from enslavement
blessed—fortunate, favored by God, happy

The truth sets us free

You will *know* the truth, and the truth will *set you free*.

—JOHN 8:32

know—recognize, understand
set you free—liberate you, free you from bondage

We are free from the law

There is *now* no *condemnation* for those who are in Christ Jesus, because through Christ Jesus the law of the Spirit of life *set me free* from the law of sin and death.

—ROMANS 8:1-2

now—at the present time
condemnation—judging one guilty of wrongdoing
set me free—liberated me, freed me

The Spirit brings freedom

The Lord is the Spirit, and where the Spirit of the Lord is, there is *freedom.*

—2 CORINTHIANS 3:17

freedom—liberty, freedom from enslavement

We may approach God with freedom

In him and through faith in him we may approach God with *freedom* and confidence.

—EPHESIANS 3:12

freedom—openness, frankness

Life

You need not worry about your life

Do not *worry* about your life, what you will eat or drink; or about your body, what you will wear. Is not life more important than food, and the body more important than clothes? Look at the birds of the air; they do not sow or reap or store away in barns, and yet your heavenly Father feeds them. Are you not much more valuable than they?

—MATTHEW 6:25-26

worry—have anxiety, be concerned

Take to God your plans and failures,
Any time and anywhere.
No one ever goes unanswered,
For He answers every prayer.

Mary Bernstecher

Jesus satisfies spiritual hunger in life

Jesus declared, "I am the bread of life. He who comes to me will *never* go hungry, and he who *believes in* me will never be thirsty."

—JOHN 6:35

never—absolutely never

believes in—trusts in, puts faith in, relies on

In Jesus we have the light of life

I am the light of the world. Whoever follows me will never walk in darkness, but will have the light of life.

—JOHN 8:12

God has given us eternal life in Jesus

This is the testimony: God has given us eternal life, and this life is in his Son. He who has the Son has life; he who does not have the Son of God does not have life.

—1 JOHN 5:11-12 (see also JOHN 3:16)

The mind controlled by the Spirit is life and peace

The mind of sinful man is death, but the mind controlled by the Spirit is life and *peace.*

—ROMANS 8:6

peace—tranquility, serenity

Because of Jesus, we can live a new life

We were therefore buried with him through baptism into death in order that, just as Christ was raised from the dead through the glory of the Father, we too may live a new life.

—ROMANS 6:4

Our lives will never end

Jesus said to her, "I am the resurrection and the life. He who *believes in* me will live, even though he dies; and whoever lives and *believes in* me will never die."

—JOHN 11:25-26

believes in—trusts in, puts faith in, relies on

Loneliness

Christ is always with us

Surely I am with you *always*, to the very end of the age.

—MATTHEW 28:20

always—perpetually, neverendingly, in all circumstances

God is always with us

God is our *refuge* and *strength*, an ever-present *help* in trouble.

—PSALM 46:1

refuge—shelter
strength—stronghold, fortification
help—support, ally

God heals the brokenhearted

He heals the brokenhearted and *binds up* their *wounds*.

—PSALM 147:3

binds up—bandages, wraps up
wounds—sorrows, griefs, pains

Nothing can separate us from the love of Christ

I am convinced that neither death nor life, neither angels nor demons, neither the present nor the future, nor any powers, neither height nor depth, nor anything else in all creation, will be able to *separate us from* the *love* of God that is in Christ Jesus our Lord.

—ROMANS 8:38-39

separate us from—divide us from, set us apart from

love—active love

Longing

God fulfills the desires of those who fear Him

He fulfills the desires of those who *fear* him; he hears their cry and saves them.

—PSALM 145:19

fear—worshipfully fear, show reverence to

Delight in the Lord, and He will give you your desires

Delight yourself in the LORD and he will give you the desires of your heart.

—PSALM 37:4

delight yourself—take your joy in

The Lord withholds nothing good from those whose walk is blameless

The LORD God is a sun and shield; the LORD bestows favor and honor; no good thing does he withhold from those whose walk is *blameless.*

—PSALM 84:11

blameless—unblemished, without defect

Dependence on the Spirit brings victory over unholy desires

Live by the Spirit, and you will not *gratify* the desires of the sinful nature.

—GALATIANS 5:16

live by—habitually walk in dependence on
gratify—fulfill

The desires of the world will pass away

The world and its *desires* pass away, but the man who does the will of God lives forever.

—1 JOHN 2:17

desires—longings, cravings, lusts

Lord Jesus

Those who believe in the Lord Jesus are saved

Believe in the Lord Jesus, and you will be *saved*—you and your household.

—ACTS 16:31

believe in—trust in, put faith in, rely on
saved—rescued, delivered

We have peace with God through the Lord Jesus

Since we have been *justified* through faith, we have *peace* with God through our Lord Jesus Christ.

—ROMANS 5:1

justified—declared righteous
peace—harmony, tranquility

We are sanctified and justified in the Lord Jesus

You were washed, you were *sanctified*, you were *justified* in the name of the Lord Jesus Christ and by the Spirit of our God.

—1 CORINTHIANS 6:11

sanctified—set apart
justified—declared righteous

Confess Jesus as Lord, and you will be saved

If you *confess* with your mouth, "Jesus is Lord," and believe in your heart that God raised him from the dead, you will be *saved*. For it is with your heart that you believe and are *justified*, and it is with your mouth that you confess and are saved.

—ROMANS 10:9-10

confess—declare, admit, acknowledge, agree
saved—rescued, delivered
justified—declared righteous

Every tongue will confess Jesus as Lord

God exalted him to the highest place and gave him the name that is above every name, that at the name of Jesus every knee should bow, in heaven and on earth and under the earth, and every tongue *confess* that Jesus Christ is Lord, to the glory of God the Father.

—PHILIPPIANS 2:9-11

confess—openly confess, admit, consent

Love for God and Jesus

Those who love Jesus are loved by the Father

Whoever has my commands and *obeys* them, he is the one who *loves* me. He who *loves* me will be loved by my Father, and I too will love him and show myself to him.

—JOHN 14:21

obeys—guards, observes, keeps
loves—actively loves

Love and obedience lead to fellowship

If anyone *loves* me, he will *obey* my teaching. My Father will love him, and we will come to him and make our *home* with him.

—JOHN 14:23

loves—actively loves
obey—keep, guard, observe
home—dwelling place, abode

God rescues those who love Him

"Because he loves me," says the LORD, "I will *rescue* him; I will *protect* him, for he acknowledges my name."

—PSALM 91:14

rescue—deliver, bring to safety
protect—keep safe

His love has no limit,
His grace has no measure,
His power has no boundary
known unto men:
For out of His infinite riches in Jesus
He giveth, and giveth, and giveth again.

Annie Johnson Flint

A wonderful destiny awaits those who love God

No eye has *seen*, no ear has heard, no mind has conceived what God has prepared for those who *love* him.

—1 CORINTHIANS 2:9

seen—perceived
love—actively love

Love of God

God's love and compassion never fail

Because of the LORD's great *love* we are not consumed, for his *compassions* never *fail.* They are *new* every morning.

—LAMENTATIONS 3:22-23

love—loyal love, faithful devotion

compassions—mercies

fail—cease, perish, deplete

new—refreshed

God proved His love for us

God *demonstrates* his own *love* for us in this: While we were still *sinners*, Christ died for us.

—ROMANS 5:8

demonstrates—proves

love—actively love

sinners—complete moral failures

Our salvation is rooted in God's love

For God so *loved* the world that he gave his one and only Son, that whoever *believes in* him shall not *perish* but have eternal life.

—JOHN 3:16 (see also EPHESIANS 2:4-7)

loved—actively loved

believes in—trusts in, puts faith in, relies on

perish—come to destruction

Nothing can separate us from God's love

I am convinced that neither death nor life, neither angels nor demons, neither the present nor the future, nor any powers, neither height nor depth, nor anything else in all creation, will be able to *separate us* from the *love* of God that is in Christ Jesus our Lord.

—ROMANS 8:38-39

separate us—divide us, set us apart
love—active love

God's love is everlastingly with those who fear Him

From everlasting to everlasting the LORD's *love* is with those who *fear* him.

—PSALM 103:17

love—loyal love, faithful devotion
fear—worshipfully fear, show reverence to

L

Love of Others

God lives in the one who loves

Since God so *loved* us, we also ought to love one another. No one has ever seen God; but if we love one another, God *lives* in us and his love is made complete in us.

—1 JOHN 4:11-12

loved—actively loved
lives—dwells, abides, remains

Whoever loves lives in the light

Whoever *loves* his brother *lives* in the light, and there is nothing in him to make him stumble.

—1 JOHN 2:10

loves—actively loves
lives—dwells, remains, abides

God is pleased when you do good to others

Do not forget to do good and to share with others, for with such sacrifices God is pleased.

—HEBREWS 13:16

Lust

The world and its desires are passing away

The world and its *desires* pass away, but the man who does the will of God lives forever.

—1 JOHN 2:17

desires—longings, cravings, lusts

We were rescued from the world and its lusts

All of us also lived among them at one time, gratifying the cravings of our sinful nature and following its desires and thoughts. Like the rest, we were by nature objects of wrath. But because of his great love for us, God, who is *rich* in *mercy*, made us alive with Christ even when we were dead in transgressions—it is by *grace* you have been saved.

—EPHESIANS 2:3-5 (see also TITUS 3:3-5)

rich—wealthy

mercy—compassion, pity

grace—unmerited favor

God can deliver you from any temptation

No *temptation* has *seized* you except what is common to man. And God is faithful; he will not let you be tempted beyond what you can *bear*. But when you are tempted, he will also provide a *way out* so that you can *stand up* under it.

—1 CORINTHIANS 10:13

temptation—trial, enticement to sin

seized—laid hold of, overtaken

bear—endure, resist

way out—means of escape

stand up—endure, bear up

Living in dependence on the Spirit brings victory

Live by the Spirit, and you will not *gratify* the desires of the sinful nature.

—GALATIANS 5:16

live by—habitually walk in dependence on

gratify—fulfill

Throw yourself headlong on to the word and promises of God, and dare to abandon yourself to the keeping and saving power of the Lord Jesus. If you have ever trusted a precious interest in the hands of any earthly friend, I conjure you, trust yourself now and all your spiritual interests in the hands of your Heavenly Friend, and never, never, *never* allow yourself to doubt again.

Hannah Whitall Smith

M

Maturity

God is working in us to bring us to maturity

It is God who *works in you* to *will* and to act according to his good purpose.

—PHILIPPIANS 2:13

works in you—energizes you, produces in you

will—desire, wish

God will one day bring His work in us to completion

He who began a good *work* in you will carry it on to *completion* until the day of Christ Jesus.

—PHILIPPIANS 1:6

work—activity, task, deed, job
completion—perfection, the finish

We are being transformed into Christ's likeness

We, who with unveiled faces all reflect the Lord's glory, are being *transformed* into his *likeness* with ever-increasing glory, which comes from the Lord, who is the Spirit.

—2 CORINTHIANS 3:18

transformed—changed in form, transfigured
likeness—image, portrait

Our renewed minds can discern the will of God

Do not *conform* any longer to the pattern of this world, but be *transformed* by the renewing of your mind. Then you will be able to test and approve what God's will is—his good, pleasing and perfect will.

—ROMANS 12:2

conform—pattern after, fashion after, mold after
transformed—changed in form, molded

Meditation

Those who meditate on God's Word prosper

Blessed is the man who does not walk in the counsel of the wicked or stand in the way of sinners or sit in the seat of mockers. But his *delight* is in the law of the LORD, and on his law he meditates day and night. He is like a tree planted by streams of water, which yields its fruit in season and whose leaf does not wither. Whatever he does *prospers*.

—PSALM 1:1-3

blessed—happy, joyful, favored by God
delight—pleasure, desire
prospers—succeeds, prevails

Do not let this Book of the Law *depart* from your mouth; *meditate* on it day and night, so that you may be careful to do everything written in it. Then you will be prosperous and successful.

—JOSHUA 1:8

depart—leave, be removed
meditate—mutter silently to yourself

Meekness

The humble will be exalted

Whoever exalts himself will be humbled, and whoever humbles himself will be *exalted.*

—MATTHEW 23:12

exalted—lifted up, elevated

The humble will be lifted up

Humble yourselves before the Lord, and he will *lift you up.*

—JAMES 4:10 (see also 1 PETER 5:6)

lift you up—exalt you, elevate you

The Lord sustains the humble

The LORD sustains the humble but casts the wicked to the ground.

—PSALM 147:6

Becoming humble like a child yields greatness

I tell you the truth, unless you change and become like little children, you will never enter the kingdom of heaven. Therefore, whoever humbles himself like this child is the greatest in the kingdom of heaven.

—MATTHEW 18:3-4

The humble are crowned with salvation

The LORD *takes delight in* his people; he *crowns* the humble with salvation.

—PSALM 149:4

takes delight in—is pleased with
crowns—adorns, endows, honors

The Lord guides the humble

He guides the humble in what is right and teaches them his way.

—PSALM 25:9

Mental Distress

The Lord will sustain us in our troubles

Cast your *cares* on the LORD and he will *sustain* you.

—PSALM 55:22

cast—throw, hurl
cares—burdens
sustain—uphold, support, bear up

God did not give us a spirit of timidity

God did not give us a spirit of *timidity*, but a spirit of *power*, of love and of self-discipline.

—2 TIMOTHY 1:7

timidity—cowardice
power—ability

It is God's will that I should cast
On Him my care each day.
He also bids me not to cast
My confidence away.
But oh, I am so foolish
That when taken unawares,
I cast away my confidence
and carry all my cares.

T. Baird

Turning anxieties over to God yields perfect peace

Do not be *anxious* about anything, but in everything, by prayer and *petition*, with thanksgiving, present your requests to God. And the *peace* of God, which *transcends* all understanding, will *guard* your hearts and your minds in Christ Jesus.

M

—PHILIPPIANS 4:6-7

anxious—worried, concerned, fretful
petition—definite requests
peace—tranquility, serenity
transcends—surpasses, exceeds
guard—shield

Christ gives us rest

Come to me, all you who are *weary* and *burdened*, and I will give you *rest*.

—MATTHEW 11:28

weary—tired, labored
burdened—weighted down
rest—refreshment, relief

A love for God's Word yields peace

Great *peace* have they who love your law, and nothing can make them stumble.

—PSALM 119:165

peace—tranquility, serenity

God heals the brokenhearted

He heals the brokenhearted and *binds up* their *wounds.*

—PSALM 147:3

binds up—bandages, wraps up
wounds—sorrows, griefs, pains

Mercy

The Lord's mercy is abundant

The Lord is full of compassion and mercy.

—JAMES 5:11

God is rich in mercy

Because of his great *love* for us, God, who is *rich* in *mercy,* made us alive with Christ even when we were dead in transgressions—it is by *grace* you have been saved.

—EPHESIANS 2:4-5

love—active love
rich—wealthy
mercy—compassion, pity
grace—unmerited favor

God has mercy on those who fear Him

His mercy extends to those who *fear* him, from generation to generation.

—LUKE 1:50

fear—worshipfully fear, show reverence to

God has compassion on those who fear Him

As a father has *compassion* on his children, so the LORD has *compassion* on those who fear him.

—PSALM 103:13

compassion—mercy

God saved us because of His mercy

He *saved* us, not because of righteous things we had done, but because of his *mercy.* He saved us through the washing of *rebirth* and renewal by the Holy Spirit.

—TITUS 3:5

saved—rescued, delivered
mercy—compassion, pity, kindness
rebirth—regeneration

Money

We need not love money, for God will never forsake us

Keep your lives free from the love of money and be content with what you have, because God has said, "*Never* will I leave you; *never* will I *forsake* you."

—HEBREWS 13:5

never—absolutely never
forsake—abandon, leave

God will meet all our needs

My God will *meet* all your needs according to his glorious riches in Christ Jesus.

—PHILIPPIANS 4:19

meet—liberally fulfill, complete

Do not *worry* about your life, what you will eat or drink; or about your body, what you will wear. Is not life more important than food, and the body more important than clothes? Look at the birds of the air; they do not sow or reap or store away in barns, and yet your heavenly Father feeds them. Are you not much more valuable than they?

—MATTHEW 6:25-26

worry—have anxiety, be concerned

N

Need

N

God will meet all our needs

My God will *meet* all your needs according to his glorious riches in Christ Jesus.

—PHILIPPIANS 4:19

meet—liberally fulfill, complete

God satisfies our needs

He *satisfies* the thirsty and fills the hungry with good things.

—PSALM 107:9

satisfies—satiates, fills and overfills

God provides food

He provides food for those who *fear* him.

—PSALM 111:5

fear—worshipfully fear, show reverence to

The Lord delivers the needy

He will *deliver* the needy who cry out, the *afflicted* who have no one to help.

—PSALM 72:12

deliver—rescue, save
afflicted—oppressed

Seek God's kingdom first, and God will meet our needs

Do not worry, saying, "What shall we eat?" or "What shall we drink?" or "What shall we wear?" For the pagans run after all these things, and your heavenly Father knows that you need them. But *seek first* his kingdom and his righteousness, and all these things will be given to you as well.

—MATTHEW 6:31-33

seek—strive for, look for, desire
first—above all, earlier

God gives us what we need to do good

God is able to make all *grace abound* to you, so that in all things at all times, having all that you need, you will *abound* in every good work.

—2 CORINTHIANS 9:8

grace—unmerited favor, kindness
abound—overflow, have an excess amount

God gives us what we need for life and godliness

His divine *power* has given us everything we need for life and *godliness* through our knowledge of him who called us by his own glory and goodness.

—2 PETER 1:3

power—ability
godliness—piety

Be still, the morning comes,
The night will end;
Trust thou in Christ thy Light,
Thy faithful Friend.
and know that He is God,
Whose perfect will
Works all things for thy good:
Look up—be still.

Florence Wills

New Life

We are new creatures in Christ

If anyone is in Christ, he is a *new creation*; the old has *gone*, the *new* has come!

—2 CORINTHIANS 5:17

new creation—altogether new
gone—passed away, come to an end, disappeared
new—fresh

We have a new life in Jesus

We were therefore buried with him through baptism into death in order that, just as Christ was raised from the dead through the glory of the Father, we too may live a new life.

—ROMANS 6:4

Those who hope in the Lord will renew their strength

Those who *hope* in the LORD will *renew* their strength. They will *soar* on wings like eagles; they will run and not grow weary, they will walk and not be faint.

—ISAIAH 40:31

hope—wait for, look for
renew—replace, refresh
soar—be lifted up, exalted

Our bodies may age, but our spirits are renewed daily

We do not *lose heart.* Though outwardly we are *wasting away,* yet inwardly we are *being renewed* day by day.

—2 CORINTHIANS 4:16

lose heart—give up, become discouraged, become wearied
wasting away—progressively decaying
being renewed—continually renewed

O

Obedience

God's love is made complete in the one who obeys

If anyone *obeys* his word, God's love is truly made *complete* in him. This is how we *know* we are in him.

—1 JOHN 2:5

obeys—keeps, guards, observes
complete—perfect
know—recognize, understand

Obedience brings the blessing of fellowship with God

If anyone *loves* me, he will *obey* my teaching. My Father will love him, and we will come to him and make our *home* with him.

—JOHN 14:23

loves—actively loved
obey—keep, guard, observe
home—dwelling place, abode

God answers prayer when we obey Him

We have *confidence* before God and receive from him anything we ask, because we *obey* his commands and do what pleases him.

—1 JOHN 3:21-22

confidence—boldness, openness, frankness
obey—observe, guard, keep

Obedience yields greatness in the kingdom

Anyone who *breaks* one of the *least* of these commandments and teaches others to do the same will be called *least* in the kingdom of heaven, but whoever practices and teaches these commands will be called great in the kingdom of heaven.

—MATTHEW 5:19

breaks—does away with, relaxes
least—most trivial

Those who do God's will are members of His family

Whoever *does* the *will* of my Father in heaven is my brother and sister and mother.

—MATTHEW 12:50

does—practices
will—desire, decision

Those who obey Jesus never permanently die

I tell you the truth, if anyone *keeps* my word, he will never *see* death.

—JOHN 8:51

keeps—guards, obeys, observes
see—experience

> Let us wrap ourselves in the warm garments of His promises.
>
> *Charles Spurgeon*

P

Patience

You will reap a harvest

Let us not become *weary* in doing good, for at the proper time we will reap a harvest if we do not *give up.*

—GALATIANS 6:9

weary—discouraged, disheartened
give up—collapse in weariness

You will receive a crown of life

Blessed is the man who *perseveres* under trial, because when he has stood the test, he will receive the crown of life that God has promised to those who love him.

—JAMES 1:12

perseveres—stands firm, endures

Those who persevere will receive what God promised

You need to *persevere* so that when you have done the will of God, you will *receive* what he has promised.

—HEBREWS 10:36

persevere—patiently endure
receive—be rewarded with

The Lord is patient regarding salvation

The Lord is not *slow* in keeping his promise, as some understand slowness. He is *patient* with you, not wanting anyone to perish, but everyone to come to *repentance.*

—2 PETER 3:9

slow—delaying, hesitating
patient—forbearing, longsuffering
repentance—change of mind, change of attitudes

Peace

Peacemakers are blessed

Blessed are the *peacemakers,* for they will be called sons of God.

—MATTHEW 5:9

blessed—happy, joyful, favored by God
peacemakers—reconcilers

Turning anxieties over to God yields perfect peace

Do not be *anxious* about anything, but in everything, by prayer and *petition,* with thanksgiving, present your requests to God. And the *peace* of God, which *transcends* all understanding, will *guard* your hearts and your minds in Christ Jesus.

—PHILIPPIANS 4:6-7

anxious—worried, concerned, fretful
petition—definite requests
peace—tranquility, serenity
transcends—surpasses, exceeds
guard—shield

The mind focused on God has perfect peace

You will keep in perfect *peace* him whose mind is steadfast, because he trusts in you.

—ISAIAH 26:3

peace—tranquility, serenity

Christ gives us peace

Peace I leave with you; my *peace* I give you. I do not give to you as the world gives. Do not let your hearts be *troubled* and do not be *afraid.*

—JOHN 14:27

peace—tranquility, serenity
troubled—disturbed, terrified, thrown into confusion
afraid—timid, cowardly

A love for God's Word yields peace

Great *peace* have they who love your law, and nothing can make them stumble.

—PSALM 119:165

peace—tranquility, serenity

The mind controlled by the Spirit is life and peace

The mind of sinful man is death, but the mind controlled by the Spirit is life and *peace.*

—ROMANS 8:6

peace—tranquility, serenity

Persecution

Those persecuted for righteousness are blessed

Blessed are those who are *persecuted* because of righteousness, for theirs is the kingdom of heaven.

—MATTHEW 5:10

blessed—happy, joyful, favored by God
persecuted—harassed, oppressed

Those persecuted for following Jesus are blessed

Blessed are you when people *insult* you, *persecute* you and falsely say all kinds of evil against you because of me. Rejoice and be glad, because great is your reward in heaven.

—MATTHEW 5:11-12

blessed—happy, joyful, favored by God
insult—denounce, rebuke
persecute—harass, oppress

Nothing can separate us from the love of Christ

I am convinced that neither death nor life, neither angels nor demons, neither the present nor the future, nor any powers, neither height nor depth, nor anything else in all creation, will be able to *separate us* from the *love* of God that is in Christ Jesus our Lord.

—ROMANS 8:38-39

separate us—divide us, set us apart
love—active love

We are blessed for suffering for what is right

Even if you should suffer for what is right, you are *blessed*.

—1 PETER 3:14

blessed—happy, joyful, favored by God

We are blessed when insulted for serving Christ

If you are *insulted* because of the name of Christ, you are *blessed*, for the Spirit of glory and of God rests on you.

—1 PETER 4:14

insulted—rebuked, denounced
blessed—happy, joyful, favored by God

> Firm are his promises,
> and strong his hand.
>
> *Isaac Watts*

Perseverance

Perseverance yields the crown of life

Blessed is the man who *perseveres* under trial, because when he has stood the test, he will receive the crown of life that God has promised to those who love him.

—JAMES 1:12

perseveres—stands firm, endures

Persevere, and you'll receive what God has promised

You need to *persevere* so that when you have done the will of God, you will *receive* what he has promised.

—HEBREWS 10:36

persevere—patiently endure
receive—be rewarded with

Suffering produces perseverance

We also *rejoice in* our *sufferings*, because we know that suffering produces *perseverance*.

—ROMANS 5:3

rejoice in—boast about, glory in
sufferings—troubles, distresses, tribulations
perseverance—patient endurance

Those who persevere will reap a harvest

Let us not become *weary* in doing good, for at the proper time we will reap a harvest if we do not *give up*.

—GALATIANS 6:9

weary—discouraged, disheartened
give up—collapse in weariness

Prayer

Ask, and it will be given to you

Ask and it will be given to you; *seek* and you will find; *knock* and the door will be opened to you. For everyone who asks receives; he who seeks finds; and to him who knocks, the door will be opened.

—MATTHEW 7:7-8 (see also LUKE 11:9-10)

ask—keep on asking
seek—keep on seeking
knock—keep on knocking

Pray in Jesus' name, and He will answer

I will do whatever you ask in my name, so that the Son may bring *glory* to the Father. You may ask me for anything in my name, and I will do it.

—JOHN 14:13-14

glory—praise, honor

God answers prayer when we obey

We have *confidence* before God and receive from him anything we ask, because we *obey* his commands and do what pleases him.

—1 JOHN 3:21-22

confidence—boldness, openness, frankness

obey—observe, guard, keep

God answers prayer when we believe

I tell you the truth, if anyone says to this mountain, "Go, throw yourself into the sea," and does not *doubt* in his heart but believes that what he says will happen, it will be done for him. Therefore I tell you, whatever you ask for in prayer, believe that you have received it, and it will be yours.

—MARK 11:23-24 (see also MATTHEW 21:22)

doubt—hesitate, waver

He is faithful to His promises,
and gracious to His saints; He will not
turn away from His people.

Charles Spurgeon

God answers the prayers of the righteous

The eyes of the Lord are on the *righteous* and his ears are attentive to their prayer, but the face of the Lord *is against* those who do evil.

—1 PETER 3:12

righteous—upright, in a right standing with God

is against—opposes, resists, frustrates

God answers prayer when we abide in Christ

If you *remain* in me and my words *remain* in you, ask whatever you wish, and it will be given you.

—JOHN 15:7

remain—abide, dwell, live

God answers prayers that are in accordance with His will

This is the *confidence* we have in approaching God: that if we ask anything according to his will, he hears us. And if we *know* that he hears us—whatever we ask—we *know* that we have what we asked of him.

—1 John 5:14-15

confidence—bold assurance
know—know with certainty and assurance

God answers prayer when two or more agree

If two of you on earth *agree* about *anything* you ask for, it will be done for you by my Father in heaven. For where two or three come together in my name, there am I with them.

—Matthew 18:19-20

agree—are in harmony
anything—anything and everything

Presence of God

P

God will never leave us

Never will I leave you; *never* will I *forsake* you.

—Hebrews 13:5

never—absolutely never
forsake—abandon, leave

Christ is always with us

Surely I am with you *always*, to the very end of the age.

—Matthew 28:20

always—perpetually, neverendingly, in all circumstances

God will draw near to those who draw near to Him

Come near to God and he will come near to you.

—JAMES 4:8

We have fellowship when we walk in the light

If we *walk* in the light, as he is in the light, we have *fellowship* with one another, and the blood of Jesus, his Son, purifies us from all sin.

—1 JOHN 1:7

walk—conduct our lives

fellowship—sharing

Christ will fellowship upon invitation

Here I am! I stand at the door and knock. If anyone *hears* my voice and opens the door, I will come in and eat with him, and he with me.

—REVELATION 3:20

hears—pays attention, understands, obeys

Pride

God gives grace to the humble

All of you, *clothe* yourselves with humility toward one another, because, "God *opposes* the proud but gives *grace* to the humble." Humble yourselves, therefore, under God's mighty hand, that he may *lift you up* in due time.

—1 PETER 5:5-6 (see also JAMES 4:6)

clothe—adorn, cover

opposes—resists

grace—unmerited favor

lift you up—exalt you, elevate you

Those who exalt themselves will be humbled

Whoever exalts himself will be humbled, and whoever humbles himself will be *exalted.*

—MATTHEW 23:12 (see also JAMES 4:10; 1 PETER 5:6)

exalted—lifted up, elevated

Becoming humble like a child yields greatness

I tell you the truth, unless you change and become like little children, you will never enter the kingdom of heaven. Therefore, whoever humbles himself like this child is the greatest in the kingdom of heaven.

—MATTHEW 18:3-4

Following the humble Jesus yields rest

Take my yoke upon you and learn from me, for I am *gentle* and *humble* in heart, and you will find *rest* for your souls.

—MATTHEW 11:29

gentle—meek
humble—lowly
rest—refreshment

Priorities

Seek God's kingdom first, and He will provide basic needs

Seek first his kingdom and his righteousness, and all these things will be given to you as well.

—MATTHEW 6:33

seek—strive for, look for, desire
first—above all, earlier

Whoever loses his life for Jesus will find it

Whoever wants to save his life will lose it, but whoever loses his life for me will save it. What good is it for a man to gain the whole world, and yet lose or forfeit his very self?

—LUKE 9:24-25

> Only trust the Savior's promise,
> Do His will, whate'er it be;
> Then our faith will hear Him saying,
> "Come and find a rest in Me."
>
> *Fanny Crosby*

Protection

God is our shield and rampart

P

He will *cover* you with his feathers, and under his wings you will find refuge; his *faithfulness* will be your shield and rampart. You will not fear the terror of night, nor the arrow that flies by day, nor the pestilence that stalks in the darkness, nor the plague that destroys at midday.

—PSALM 91:4-6 (see also PSALM 18:30)

cover—overshadow, conceal

faithfulness—trustworthiness, reliability

God rescues those who love Him

"Because he loves me," says the LORD, "I will *rescue* him; I will *protect him*, for he acknowledges my name."

—PSALM 91:14

rescue—deliver, bring to safety

protect him—keep him safe

The Lord protects His faithful ones

The LORD *loves* the just and will not *forsake* his faithful ones. They will be *protected* forever, but the offspring of the wicked will be cut off.

—PSALM 37:28

loves—loves like a friend

forsake—desert, abandon

protected—guarded, watched over

God protects us from Satan

The Lord is *faithful*, and he will strengthen and protect you from the evil one.

—2 THESSALONIANS 3:3

faithful—trustworthy, dependable, reliable

God protects us from disaster

If you make the Most High your dwelling—even the LORD, who is my *refuge*—then no *harm* will befall you, no *disaster* will come near your tent.

—PSALM 91:9-10

refuge—shelter

harm—trouble, wickedness

disaster—plague, blow, scourge

The Lord will watch over you

The LORD will keep you from all harm—he will *watch* over your life; the LORD will *watch* over your coming and going both now and forevermore.

—PSALM 121:7-8 (see also PSALM 145:20)

watch—observe, guard

Providence of God

The Lord's kingdom rules over all

The LORD has *established* his throne in heaven, and his kingdom *rules* over all.

—PSALM 103:19

established—set in place, prepared
rules—governs, has dominion

The sovereign Lord rules

The Sovereign LORD comes with power, and his arm *rules* for him.

—ISAIAH 40:10

rules—governs, controls, maintains dominion

Even in our troubles, God is working for our good

We know that in all things God works for the *good* of those who *love* him, who have been called according to his purpose.

—ROMANS 8:28

good—positive good, moral good
love—actively love

Provision

God will meet all our needs

My God will *meet* all your needs according to his glorious riches in Christ Jesus.

—PHILIPPIANS 4:19

meet—liberally fulfill, complete

God provides for those who fear Him

He provides food for those who *fear* him.

—PSALM 111:5

fear—worshipfully fear, show reverence to

Put God first, and temporal needs will be met

Seek first his kingdom and his righteousness, and all these things will be given to you as well.

—MATTHEW 6:33

seek—strive for, look for, desire
first—above all, earlier

God provides for our hunger

He *satisfies* the thirsty and fills the hungry with good things.

—PSALM 107:9

satisfies—satiates, fills and overfills

God will take care of you

If that is how God clothes the grass of the field, which is here today, and tomorrow is thrown into the fire, how much more will he clothe you, O you of little faith!

—LUKE 12:28

Punishment

God lovingly disciplines Christians

"The Lord *disciplines* those he *loves*, and he *punishes* everyone he *accepts* as a son." *Endure* hardship as discipline; God is treating you as sons.

—HEBREWS 12:6-7

disciplines—trains, instructs, educates
loves—actively loves
punishes—scourges, chastises
accepts—receives, welcomes
endure—patiently endure

God punishes the evil with everlasting destruction

They will be punished with everlasting *destruction* and shut out from the presence of the Lord and from the majesty of his power.

—2 THESSALONIANS 1:9

destruction—ruin

Purification

God will cleanse the stain of sin from your soul

Though your *sins* are like scarlet, they shall be as *white* as snow; though they are red as crimson, they shall be like wool.

—ISAIAH 1:18

sins—actions contrary to the law of God

white—whitened, spotless, purified

The blood of Christ cleanses us

How much more, then, will the blood of Christ, who through the eternal Spirit offered himself unblemished to God, *cleanse* our consciences from acts that lead to death, so that we may serve the living God!

—HEBREWS 9:14

cleanse—purify, make clean

We are purified from all sin

If we *walk* in the light, as he is in the light, we have *fellowship* with one another, and the blood of Jesus, his Son, purifies us from all sin.

—1 JOHN 1:7

walk—conduct our lives

fellowship—sharing

God cleanses us when we confess

If we *confess* our sins, he is faithful and just and will *forgive* us our sins and purify us from all unrighteousness.

—1 JOHN 1:9

confess—admit, agree, acknowledge
forgive—pardon, remit, cancel

> Thy promises are true,
> Thy grace is ever new.
>
> *Isaac Watts*

Purity comes from following God's Word

How can a young man keep his way *pure*? By living according to your word.

—PSALM 119:9

pure—morally pure, clean

The pure in heart will see God

Blessed are the *pure* in heart, for they will see God.

—MATTHEW 5:8

blessed—happy, joyful, favored by God
pure—clean, innocent

Pursuit of God

Seek God's kingdom first, and He will provide basic needs

Seek first his kingdom and his righteousness, and all these things will be given to you as well.

—MATTHEW 6:33

seek—strive for, look for, desire
first—above all, earlier

Seek God with all your heart and you will find Him

You will seek me and find me when you seek me with *all* your heart.

—JEREMIAH 29:13

all—the entirety of, the totality of

The Lord is good to the one who seeks Him

The Lord is good to those whose hope is in him, to the one who *seeks* him.

—LAMENTATIONS 3:25

seeks—seeks, inquires of, consults with

Those who seek the Lord lack no good thing

The lions may grow weak and hungry, but those who seek the LORD lack no good thing.

—PSALM 34:10

God rewards those who earnestly seek Him

Without faith *it is impossible* to *please* God, because anyone who comes to him must believe that he exists and that he rewards those who *earnestly* seek him.

—HEBREWS 11:6

it is impossible—one is powerless
please—truly please, be satisfactory to
earnestly—diligently

Seek and you will find

Ask and it will be given to you; *seek* and you will find; *knock* and the door will be opened to you. For everyone who asks receives; he who seeks finds; and to him who knocks, the door will be opened.

—MATTHEW 7:7-8 (see also LUKE 11:9-10)

ask—keep on asking
seek—keep on seeking
knock—keep on knocking

Q-R

Rapture

We will all be changed

We will not all *sleep*, but we will all be changed—in a *flash*, in the twinkling of an eye, at the last trumpet. For the trumpet will sound, the dead will be raised *imperishable*, and we will be changed. For the perishable must clothe itself with the imperishable, and the mortal with immortality.

—1 CORINTHIANS 15:51-53

sleep—sleep in death
flash—indivisible moment
imperishable—immortal, lasting forever

We will meet the Lord in the clouds

The Lord himself will come down from heaven, with a loud command, with the voice of the archangel and with the trumpet call of God, and the dead in Christ will rise first. After that, we who are still alive and are left will be *caught up* together with them in the clouds to meet the Lord in the air. And so we will be with the Lord forever.

—1 THESSALONIANS 4:16-17

caught up—snatched up, carried up

Rebirth

We are born again

You have been *born again*, not of *perishable* seed, but of *imperishable*, through the living and enduring word of God.

—1 PETER 1:23

born again—born anew, born spiritually
perishable—that which does not last
imperishable—immortal, that which lasts forever

We are new creations in Christ

If anyone is in Christ, he is a *new creation*; the old has *gone*, the *new* has come!

—2 CORINTHIANS 5:17

new creation—altogether new
gone—passed away, come to an end, disappeared
new—fresh

We are saved through the washing of rebirth

He saved us, not because of righteous things we had done, but because of his mercy. He saved us through the washing of *rebirth* and renewal by the Holy Spirit.

—TITUS 3:5

rebirth—regeneration

Those who believe in Jesus are God's children

To all who received him, to those who *believed in* his name, he gave the *right* to become children of God.

—JOHN 1:12

believed in—put trust in
right—authority, power

Redemption

We were redeemed by Jesus' blood

It was not with *perishable* things such as silver or gold that you were redeemed from the *empty* way of life handed down to you from your forefathers, but with the *precious* blood of Christ, a lamb without blemish or defect.

—1 PETER 1:18-19

perishable—that which does not last
empty—futile, worthless
precious—costly, valuable

We are redeemed and forgiven

In him we have *redemption* through his blood, the *forgiveness* of sins, in accordance with the riches of God's *grace.*

—EPHESIANS 1:7

redemption—ransom, release from sin
forgiveness—pardon, cancellation of all debt
grace—unmerited favor

> He is a sovereign God with the power to accomplish all He has promised. He is a God who wants us to understand how completely He is committed to keeping His promises.
>
> *Larry Richards*

Jesus died for the sins of the whole world

He is the *atoning sacrifice* for our *sins,* and not only for ours but also for the sins of the whole world.

—1 JOHN 2:2 (see also HEBREWS 9:28)

atoning sacrifice—propitiation, basis of forgiveness
sins—wrongdoings, acts contrary to God's law

We are saved from God's wrath

Since we have now been *justified* by his blood, how much more shall we be *saved* from God's *wrath* through him!

—ROMANS 5:9

justified—declared righteous
saved—rescued, delivered
wrath—anger, displeasure, hostility

We've been brought into a new kingdom

He has rescued us from the *dominion* of darkness and brought us into the *kingdom* of the Son he loves, in whom we have redemption, the forgiveness of sins.

—COLOSSIANS 1:13-14 (see also COLOSSIANS 2:13-14)

dominion—authority, power, right to control
kingdom—royal rule

Refreshment

God refreshes the weary

I will refresh the weary and satisfy the faint.

—JEREMIAH 31:25

Christ gives us rest

Come to me, all you who are *weary* and *burdened*, and I will give you *rest.*

—MATTHEW 11:28

weary—tired, labored
burdened—weighted down
rest—refreshment, relief

Repentance brings times of refreshing

Repent, then, and turn to God, so that your sins may be *wiped out*, that times of *refreshing* may come from the Lord.

—ACTS 3:19

repent—change your mind, change your attitudes
wiped out—canceled, blotted out
refreshing—relief, relaxation

We are new creations in Christ

If anyone is in Christ, he is a *new creation*; the old has *gone*, the *new* has come!

—2 CORINTHIANS 5:17

new creation—altogether new
gone—passed away, come to an end, disappeared
new—fresh

Our spirits are renewed daily

We do not *lose heart*. Though outwardly we are *wasting away*, yet inwardly we are *being renewed* day by day.

—2 CORINTHIANS 4:16

lose heart—give up, become discouraged, become wearied
wasting away—progressively decaying
being renewed—continually renewed

Those who hope in the Lord will renew their strength

Those who *hope in* the LORD will *renew* their strength. They will *soar* on wings like eagles; they will run and not grow weary, they will walk and not be faint.

—ISAIAH 40:31

hope in—wait for, look for
renew—replace, refresh
soar—be lifted up, exalted

Repentance

Repentance leads to life

If a wicked man *turns away* from all the sins he has committed and *keeps* all my decrees and does what is just and right, he will surely *live;* he will not die. None of the offenses he has committed will be remembered against him. Because of the righteous things he has done, he will live.

—EZEKIEL 18:21-22

turns away—repents
keeps—observes, guards
live—recover, be revived

Repentance brings times of refreshing

Repent, then, and turn to God, so that your sins may be *wiped out,* that times of *refreshing* may come from the Lord.

—ACTS 3:19

repent—change your mind, change your attitudes
wiped out—canceled, blotted out
refreshing—relief, relaxation

Heaven rejoices when a sinner repents

There will be more *rejoicing* in heaven over one sinner who *repents* than over ninety-nine righteous persons who do not need to repent.

—LUKE 15:7 (see also LUKE 15:10)

rejoicing—joy, happiness, gladness
repents—changes attitudes, thoughts, and behaviors toward God

The Lord seeks all to come to repentance

The Lord is not *slow* in keeping his promise, as some understand slowness. He is *patient* with you, not wanting anyone to perish, but everyone to come to *repentance.*

—2 PETER 3:9

slow—delaying, hesitating
patient—forbearing, longsuffering
repentance—involving a change of mind and attitudes

> Thy promises, how firm they be!
> How firm our hope and comfort stands.
>
> *Isaac Watts*

Rest

Christ gives us rest

Come to me, all you who are *weary* and *burdened*, and I will give you *rest.*

—MATTHEW 11:28

weary—tired, labored
burdened—weighted down
rest—refreshment, relief

Q
R

We can rest in the secure presence of God

He who *dwells* in the shelter of the Most High will rest in the shadow of the Almighty.

—PSALM 91:1

dwells—inhabits, settles

God refreshes the weary

I will refresh the weary and satisfy the faint.

—Jeremiah 31:25

We can enjoy a perpetual Sabbath-rest

There remains, then, a Sabbath-rest for the people of God.

—Hebrews 4:9 (see also Hebrews 4:1)

Restoration

We are new creatures in Christ

If anyone is in Christ, he is a *new creation*; the old has *gone*, the *new* has come!

—2 Corinthians 5:17

new creation—altogether new

gone—passed away, come to an end, disappeared

new—fresh

The Lord lifts up those who are bowed down

The Lord *upholds* all those who fall and lifts up all who are bowed down.

—Psalm 145:14

upholds—sustains, undergirds

The God of grace will restore us

The God of all *grace*, who called you to his eternal glory in Christ, after you have suffered a little while, will himself *restore* you and make you strong, firm and steadfast.

—1 Peter 5:10

grace—unmerited favor

restore—mend, make complete

Our spirits are renewed daily

We do not *lose heart.* Though outwardly we are *wasting away*, yet inwardly we are *being renewed* day by day.

—2 CORINTHIANS 4:16

lose heart—give up, become discouraged, become wearied
wasting away—progressively decaying
being renewed—continually renewed

Those who hope in the Lord will renew their strength

Those who *hope in* the LORD will *renew* their strength. They will *soar* on wings like eagles; they will run and not grow weary, they will walk and not be faint.

—ISAIAH 40:31

hope in—wait for, look for
renew—replace, refresh
soar—be lifted up, exalted

We are brought near to God through Jesus Christ

In Christ Jesus you who once were *far away* have been brought near through the blood of Christ.

—EPHESIANS 2:13

far away—a long way off, distant

Resurrection

Those who believe in Jesus will be resurrected

Jesus said to her, "I am the resurrection and the life. He who *believes in* me will live, even though he dies; and whoever lives and *believes in* me will never die."

—JOHN 11:25-26

believes in—trusts in, puts faith in, relies on

We have a living hope of resurrection

Praise be to the God and Father of our Lord Jesus Christ! In his *great mercy* he has given us new birth into a living *hope* through the resurrection of Jesus Christ from the dead.

—1 PETER 1:3

great mercy—superabundant compassion
hope—expectation

Our mortal bodies will be enlivened

If the Spirit of him who raised Jesus from the dead is living in you, he who raised Christ from the dead will also give life to your mortal bodies through his Spirit, who lives in you.

—ROMANS 8:11

Permanent resurrection bodies await us

We know that if the earthly tent we live in is *destroyed,* we have a building from God, an eternal house in heaven, not built by human hands.

—2 CORINTHIANS 5:1

destroyed—thrown down, dissolved, abolished

My Lord never fails to honor His promises; and when we bring them to His throne, He never sends them back unanswered.

Charles Spurgeon

Our perishable bodies will be made imperishable

The body that is *sown* is *perishable*, it is raised *imperishable*; it is sown in *dishonor*, it is raised in glory; it is sown in *weakness*, it is raised in power; it is sown a natural body, it is raised a spiritual body.

—1 CORINTHIANS 15:42-44 (see also 1 CORINTHIANS 15:51-53)

sown—sown in death

perishable—does not last

imperishable—immortal, lasting forever

dishonor—shame, disgrace

weakness—infirmity, illness

Some will rise to eternal life, others to everlasting contempt

A time is coming when all who are in their graves will hear his voice and come out—those who have done good will *rise* to live, and those who have done evil will *rise* to be condemned.

—JOHN 5:28-29 (see also DANIEL 12:2)

rise—be resurrected

Reward

The Lord will reward people for the good they do

The Lord will *reward* everyone for whatever good he does, whether he is slave or free.

—EPHESIANS 6:8

reward—pay back

The Lord searches the heart to reward justly

I the LORD *search* the heart and *examine* the mind, to reward a man according to his conduct, according to what his deeds deserve.

—JEREMIAH 17:10

search—explore, probe

examine—test, try

Even small acts of kindness will be rewarded

If anyone gives even a cup of cold water to one of these little ones because he is my disciple, I tell you the truth, he will *certainly not* lose his *reward.*

—MATTHEW 10:42

certainly not—absolutely not
reward—what is paid back

Enduring persecution for following Christ brings a reward

Blessed are you when people *insult* you, *persecute* you and falsely say all kinds of evil against you because of me. Rejoice and be glad, because great is your reward in heaven.

—MATTHEW 5:11-12

blessed—happy, joyful, favored by God
insult—denounce, rebuke
persecute—harass, oppress

Persevering under trial brings a reward

Blessed is the man who *perseveres* under trial, because when he has stood the test, he will receive the crown of life that God has promised to those who love him.

—JAMES 1:12

perseveres—stands firm, patiently endures

We have an inheritance from the Lord as a reward

Whatever you do, work at it with all your heart, as working for the Lord, not for men, since you know that you will receive an inheritance from the Lord as a reward. It is the Lord Christ you are *serving.*

—COLOSSIANS 3:23-24

serving—serving as a slave

Righteousness

The Lord is righteous

The LORD is righteous in all his ways and loving toward all he has made.

—PSALM 145:17

God blesses those who walk in righteousness

The LORD God is a sun and shield; the LORD bestows favor and honor; no good thing does he withhold from those whose walk is *blameless.*

—PSALM 84:11

blameless—unblemished, without defect

Those who yearn for righteousness will be satisfied

Blessed are those who hunger and thirst for righteousness, for they will be *filled.*

—MATTHEW 5:6

blessed—happy, joyful, favored by God

filled—filled to satisfaction, filled to the full

God gives you what you need to be righteous

God is able to make all *grace abound* to you, so that in all things at all times, having all that you need, you will *abound* in every good work.

—2 CORINTHIANS 9:8

grace—unmerited favor, kindness

abound—overflow

Faith is credited as righteousness

To the man who does not *work* but trusts God who *justifies* the wicked, his faith is *credited* as righteousness.

—ROMANS 4:5 (see also ROMANS 3:22-24; 5:17)

work—work actively, work to accomplish

justifies—declares righteous

credited—reckoned, counted, regarded

> The greatness of the Promiser enhances the greatness of the promises.
>
> *A.R. Fausset*

S

Sadness

God comforts those who mourn

Blessed are those who *mourn*, for they will be *comforted.*

—MATTHEW 5:4

blessed—happy, joyful, favored by God

mourn—grieve

comforted—encouraged, exhorted

God heals the brokenhearted

He heals the brokenhearted and *binds up* their *wounds.*

—PSALM 147:3

binds up—bandages, wraps up

wounds—sorrows, griefs, pains

The Lord sustains us in our troubles

Cast your *cares* on the LORD and he will *sustain* you; he will never let the righteous fall.

—PSALM 55:22

cast—throw, hurl

cares—burdens

sustain—uphold, support, bear up

God comforts us in all our troubles

Praise be to the God and Father of our Lord Jesus Christ, the Father of *compassion* and the God of all *comfort*, who comforts us in all our *troubles*, so that we can comfort those in any trouble with the comfort we ourselves have received from God.

—2 CORINTHIANS 1:3

compassion—mercy, pity

comfort—consolation, encouragement

troubles—distresses, tribulations

God will help you

Do not fear, for I am with you; do not be dismayed, for I am your God. I will *strengthen* you and help you; I will *uphold* you with my righteous right hand.

—ISAIAH 41:10

strengthen—support, establish, harden against difficulties

uphold—take hold of, grasp firmly

Turning our anxieties over to God yields perfect peace

Do not be *anxious* about anything, but in everything, by prayer and *petition*, with thanksgiving, present your requests to God. And the *peace* of God, which *transcends* all understanding, will *guard* your hearts and your minds in Christ Jesus.

—PHILIPPIANS 4:6-7

anxious—worried, concerned, fretful
petition—definite requests
peace—tranquility, serenity
transcends—surpasses, exceeds
guard—shield

Salvation

Those who believe in Jesus receive eternal life

For God so *loved* the world that he gave his one and only Son, that whoever *believes in* him shall not *perish* but have eternal life.

—JOHN 3:16 (see also JOHN 3:36; 5:24; 6:47)

loved—actively loved
believes in—trusts in, puts faith in, relies on
perish—come to destruction

Those who believe in Jesus are God's children

To all who received him, to those who *believed in* his name, he gave the *right* to become children of God.

—JOHN 1:12

believed in—put trust in
right—authority, power

Those who believe in Jesus are saved

Believe in the Lord Jesus, and you will be *saved*—you and your household.

—ACTS 16:31

believe in—trust in, put faith in, rely on
saved—rescued, delivered

Eternal life is in the Son

This is the testimony: God has given us eternal life, and this life is in his Son. He who has the Son has life; he who does not have the Son of God does not have life.

—1 JOHN 5:11-12

Call on the name of the Lord, and you'll be saved

Everyone who calls on the name of the Lord will be saved.

—ACTS 2:21 (see also ROMANS 10:11-13)

saved—rescued, delivered

Confess, and you'll be saved

If you *confess* with your mouth, "Jesus is Lord," and believe in your heart that God raised him from the dead, you will be *saved.*

—ROMANS 10:9

confess—agree, admit, acknowledge
saved—rescued, delivered

> Three things are called precious in the Scripture: the blood of Christ is called "precious blood," 1 Peter 1:19; and faith is called "precious faith," 2 Peter 1:1; and the promises are called "precious promises," 2 Peter 1:4.
>
> *Thomas Brooks*

Salvation, Security in

God's people are sealed by the Holy Spirit

Having believed, you were *marked* in him with a *seal*, the promised Holy Spirit, who is a *deposit* guaranteeing our inheritance until the redemption of those who are God's possession.

—EPHESIANS 1:13-14

marked—stamped
seal—mark of possession, mark of identity
deposit—down payment, pledge, foretaste

Jesus prays for us

He is able to *save* completely those who come to God through him, because he always lives to *intercede* for them.

—HEBREWS 7:25

save—rescue, deliver
intercede—pray, petition

Christ will never reject any who come to Him

All that the Father gives me will come to me, and whoever comes to me I will never *drive away*.

—JOHN 6:37

drive away—drive out, send out, expel

No one can snatch believers out of God's hands

My sheep *listen to* my voice; I know them, and they follow me. I give them eternal life, and they shall *never* perish; no one can *snatch* them out of my hand. My Father, who has given them to me, is greater than all; no one can *snatch* them out of my Father's hand.

—JOHN 10:27-29

listen—understand, obey, pay attention to
never—never by any means
snatch—steal, carry off

Salvation involves an unbroken chain

For those God *foreknew* he also *predestined* to be conformed to the *likeness* of his Son, that he might be the firstborn among many brothers. And those he predestined, he also *called*; those he called, he also *justified*; those he justified, he also glorified.

—ROMANS 8:29-30

foreknew—knew beforehand
predestined—decided beforehand
likeness—image, portrait
called—summoned, invited
justified—declared righteous

Sanctification

Dependence on the Holy Spirit brings victory

Live by the Spirit, and you will not *gratify* the desires of the sinful nature.

—GALATIANS 5:16

live by—habitually walk in dependence on
gratify—fulfill

The mind controlled by the Spirit is life and peace

Those who *live according to* the sinful nature have their minds set on what that nature desires; but those who live in accordance with the Spirit have their minds set on what the Spirit desires. The mind of sinful man is death, but the mind controlled by the Spirit is life and *peace*.

—ROMANS 8:5-6

living according to—are controlled by
peace—tranquility, serenity

We are being transformed into Christ's likeness

We, who with unveiled faces all reflect the Lord's glory, are being *transformed* into his *likeness* with ever-increasing glory, which comes from the Lord, who is the Spirit.

—2 CORINTHIANS 3:18

transformed—changed in form, transfigured
likeness—image, portrait

You can be transformed by the renewing of your mind

Do not *conform* any longer to the pattern of this world, but be *transformed* by the renewing of your mind. Then you will be able to test and approve what God's will is—his good, pleasing and perfect will.

—ROMANS 12:2

conform—pattern after, fashion after, mold after
transformed—changed in form, molded

We have been sanctified in the name of Jesus Christ

You were washed, you were *sanctified*, you were *justified* in the name of the Lord Jesus Christ and by the Spirit of our God.

—1 CORINTHIANS 6:11

sanctified—set apart
justified—declared righteous

Satan

God will protect us from Satan

The Lord is *faithful*, and he will strengthen and protect you from the evil one.

—2 THESSALONIANS 3:3

faithful—trustworthy, dependable, reliable

God's armor protects us from Satan

Put on the full armor of God, so that when the day of evil comes, you may be able to *stand* your ground, and after you have done everything, to *stand*.

—EPHESIANS 6:13

stand—withstand, resist, oppose

Resist the devil, and he will flee from you

Resist the devil, and he will flee from you.

—JAMES 4:7

resist—withstand, oppose

God will crush Satan

The God of *peace* will soon *crush* Satan under your feet.

—ROMANS 16:20

peace—tranquility, serenity, well-being, welfare
crush—break, dash to pieces, destroy

God is our powerful protector

He will *cover* you with his feathers, and under his wings you will find refuge; his *faithfulness* will be your shield and rampart. You will not fear the terror of night, nor the arrow that flies by day, nor the pestilence that stalks in the darkness, nor the plague that destroys at midday.

—PSALM 91:4-6

cover—overshadow, conceal
faithfulness—trustworthiness, reliability

Satisfaction

Those who seek the Lord lack no good thing

The lions may grow weak and hungry, but those who seek the LORD lack no good thing.

—PSALM 34:10

Delight in the Lord and He will give you your desires

Delight yourself in the LORD and he will give you the desires of your heart.

—PSALM 37:4

delight yourself in—take your joy in

God satisfies the hungry and thirsty

He *satisfies* the thirsty and fills the hungry with good things.

—PSALM 107:9

satisfies—satiates, fills and overfills

Blessed are you who hunger now, for you will be satisfied. *Blessed* are you who weep now, for you will laugh.

—LUKE 6:21

blessed—happy, joyful, favored by God

I love to plead his promises,
And rest upon his word.

Isaac Watts

Those who love the Lord are satisfied with longevity

With long life will I *satisfy* him and show him my salvation.

—PSALM 91:16

satisfy—satiate to the point of overfilling

Savior

Jesus saves the lost

The Son of Man came to *seek* and to *save* what was lost.

—LUKE 19:10

seek—try to obtain, strive for

save—rescue, deliver

Those who believe in Jesus receive eternal life

For God so *loved* the world that he gave his one and only Son, that whoever *believes in* him shall not *perish* but have eternal life.

—JOHN 3:16 (see also JOHN 6:47)

loved—actively loved

believes in—trusts in, puts faith in, relies on

perish—come to destruction

Confess Jesus is Lord, and you'll be saved

If you *confess* with your mouth, "Jesus is Lord," and believe in your heart that God raised him from the dead, you will be *saved.*

—ROMANS 10:9

confess—declare, admit, acknowledge, agree

saved—rescued, delivered

The Savior will return and transform us

Our citizenship is in heaven. And we eagerly await a Savior from there, the Lord Jesus Christ, who, by the *power* that enables him to bring everything under his *control*, will *transform* our lowly bodies so that they will be like his glorious body.

—PHILIPPIANS 3:20-21

power—energy
control—subjection, subordination
transform—change the form of, fashion anew

Scripture

Scripture is inspired and leads us into truth

All Scripture is *God-breathed* and is *useful* for teaching, rebuking, correcting and training in righteousness, so that the man of God may be *thoroughly equipped* for every good work.

—2 TIMOTHY 3:16-17

God-breathed—inspired
useful—valuable, profitable
thoroughly equipped—capable of meeting all demands, proficient

Obeying God's Word brings blessing

S

The man who looks intently into the perfect law that gives *freedom*, and continues to do this, not forgetting what he has heard, but doing it—he will be *blessed* in what he does.

—JAMES 1:25

freedom—liberty, freedom from enslavement
blessed—happy, joyful, favored by God

Meditating on God's Word brings prosperity

Do not let this Book of the Law *depart* from your mouth; *meditate* on it day and night, so that you may be careful to do everything written in it. Then you will be prosperous and successful.

—JOSHUA 1:8 (see also PSALM 1:1-3)

depart—leave, be removed

meditate—mutter silently to oneself

Those who love God's Word have peace

Great *peace* have they who love your law, and nothing can make them stumble.

—PSALM 119:165

peace—tranquility, serenity

Second Coming

Every eye will witness the Second Coming

Every eye will *see* him, even those who pierced him; and all the peoples of the earth will *mourn* because of him.

—REVELATION 1:7

see—perceive, notice

mourn—beat breasts in mourning

Christ will come suddenly

As lightning that comes from the east is visible even in the west, so will be the coming of the Son of Man.

—MATTHEW 24:27

The Lord will come at an unexpected hour

Therefore *keep watch*, because you do not know on what day your Lord will come.

—MATTHEW 24:42

keep watch—be on guard

Christ will come in great glory

At that time the sign of the Son of Man will appear in the sky, and all the nations of the earth will *mourn*. They will see the Son of Man coming on the clouds of the sky, with power and great glory.

—MATTHEW 24:30

mourn—beat breasts in mourning

Christians will receive a crown at the Second Coming

When the Chief Shepherd appears, you will receive the crown of glory that will never fade away.

—1 PETER 5:4

Christ will come in judgment

Wait till the Lord comes. He will *bring to light* what is *hidden* in darkness and will *expose* the *motives* of men's hearts.

—1 CORINTHIANS 4:5

bring to light—enlighten, illuminate
hidden—secret, unseen, undisclosed
expose—disclose, display, reveal
motives—plans, purposes

Behold, I am coming soon! My *reward* is with me, and I will *give* to everyone according to what he has done.

—REVELATION 22:12 (see also MATTHEW 16:27)

reward—what is paid back, wages
give—repay, render

> The promises of God are the only sure foundation of our hope.
>
> *John Wesley*

Security

Christ will never reject any who come to Him

All that the Father gives me will come to me, and whoever comes to me I will never *drive away.*

—JOHN 6:37

drive away—drive out, send out, expel

Our inheritance is secure

In his great mercy he has given us new birth into a living hope through the resurrection of Jesus Christ from the dead, and into an inheritance that can never *perish,* spoil or fade—*kept* in heaven for you.

—1 PETER 1:3-4

perish—fade away, pass away

kept—guarded

The Holy Spirit guarantees our inheritance

It is God who makes both us and you stand firm in Christ. He anointed us, set his *seal* of ownership on us, and put his Spirit in our hearts as a *deposit,* guaranteeing what is to come.

—2 CORINTHIANS 1:21-22

seal—mark of ownership, possession, identity

deposit—down payment, pledge, foretaste

We are sealed by the Holy Spirit

Having believed, you were *marked* in him with a *seal,* the promised Holy Spirit, who is a *deposit* guaranteeing our inheritance until the redemption of those who are God's possession.

—EPHESIANS 1:13-14

marked—stamped
seal—mark of ownership, possession, identity
deposit—down payment, pledge, foretaste

Nothing can separate us from the love of God

I am convinced that neither death nor life, neither angels nor demons, neither the present nor the future, nor any powers, neither height nor depth, nor anything else in all creation, will be able to *separate us* from the *love* of God that is in Christ Jesus our Lord.

—ROMANS 8:38-39

separate us—divide us, set us apart
love—active love

We will not perish

I give them eternal life, and they shall *never* perish; no one can *snatch* them out of my hand.

—JOHN 10:28

never—never by any means
snatch—steal, carry off

Seeking God

The Lord is good to those who seek Him

The LORD is good to those whose hope is in him, to the one who *seeks* him.

—LAMENTATIONS 3:25

seeks—seeks, inquires of, consults with

We find God when we seek Him with all our hearts

You will seek me and find me when you seek me with *all* your heart.

—JEREMIAH 29:13

all—the entirety of, the totality of

God will draw near to those who draw near to Him

Come near to God and he will come near to you.

—JAMES 4:8

Those who seek the Lord find full satisfaction in Him

The lions may grow weak and hungry, but those who seek the LORD lack no good thing.

—PSALM 34:10

Self-Control

God can help you when you are tempted

Because he himself suffered when he was tempted, he is able to *help* those who are being tempted.

—HEBREWS 2:18

help—come to the aid, assist, relieve

God can deliver you from any temptation

No *temptation* has *seized* you except what is common to man. And God is faithful; he will not let you be tempted beyond what you can *bear*. But when you are tempted, he will also provide a *way out* so that you can *stand up* under it.

—1 CORINTHIANS 10:13

temptation—trial, enticement to sin

seized—laid hold of, overtaken

bear—endure, resist

way out—means of escape

stand up—endure, bear up

> God makes a promise;
> faith believes it, hope anticipates it,
> patience quietly awaits it.
>
> *Anonymous*

Self-Denial

Whoever denies himself to follow Christ will find his life

If anyone would come after me, he must *deny* himself and take up his cross and follow me. For whoever wants to save his life will lose it, but whoever loses his life for me will find it.

—MATTHEW 16:24-25

deny—disown, repudiate, lose sight of, have no regard for

If you put to death the misdeeds of the body, you will live

If you live according to the sinful nature, you will die; but if by the Spirit you put to death the misdeeds of the body, you will live.

—ROMANS 8:13

Seek God's kingdom first, and He will meet basic needs

Seek first his kingdom and his righteousness, and all these things will be given to you as well.

—MATTHEW 6:33

seek—strive for, look for, desire

first—above all, earlier

Self-Worth

We are of great worth to God

Are not two sparrows sold for a penny? Yet not one of them will fall to the ground apart from the will of your Father. And even the very hairs of your head are all numbered. So don't be afraid; you are worth more than many sparrows.

—MATTHEW 10:29-31

We are children of God

How great is the *love* the Father has lavished on us, that we should be called children of God! And that is what we are!

—1 JOHN 3:1

love—active love

We are adopted into God's family

He *predestined* us to be adopted as his sons through Jesus Christ, in accordance with his pleasure and will—to the praise of his glorious *grace*, which he has freely given us in the One he loves.

—EPHESIANS 1:5-6 (see also GALATIANS 3:26)

predestined—decided beforehand

grace—unmerited favor

We are not slaves but children and heirs of God

Because you are *sons*, God sent the Spirit of his Son into our hearts, the Spirit who calls out, "*Abba*, Father." So you are no longer a *slave*, but a son; and since you are a son, God has made you also an heir.

—GALATIANS 4:6-7 (see also ROMANS 8:14-15)

sons—endeared children

Abba—dear daddy

slave—servant

All people are equal in Christ

Here there is *no* Greek or Jew, circumcised or uncircumcised, barbarian, Scythian, slave or free, but Christ is all, and is in all.

—COLOSSIANS 3:11 (see also GALATIANS 3:8)

no—absolutely no

Service

The Lord will reward our service

Whatever you do, work at it with all your heart, as working for the Lord, not for men, since you know that you will receive an inheritance from the Lord as a reward. It is the Lord Christ you are *serving.*

—COLOSSIANS 3:23-24

serving—serving as a slave

Even small acts of service bring blessing from God

If anyone gives even a cup of cold water to one of these little ones because he is my disciple, I tell you the truth, he will *certainly not* lose his *reward.*

—MATTHEW 10:42

certainly not—absolutely not

reward—what is paid back

We can comfort others

Praise be to the God and Father of our Lord Jesus Christ, the Father of *compassion* and the God of all *comfort,* who *comforts* us in all our troubles, so that we can *comfort* those in any *trouble* with the *comfort* we ourselves have received from God. For just as the sufferings of Christ flow over into our lives, so also through Christ our *comfort* overflows.

—2 CORINTHIANS 1:3-5

compassion—mercy, pity

comfort—consolation, encouragement

trouble—distress, tribulation

Sexual Temptation

God can deliver you from any temptation

No *temptation* has *seized* you except what is common to man. And God is faithful; he will not let you be tempted beyond what you can *bear.* But when you are tempted, he will also provide a *way out* so that you can *stand up* under it.

—1 CORINTHIANS 10:13

temptation—trial, enticement to sin
seized—laid hold of, overtaken
bear—endure, resist
way out—means of escape
stand up—endure, bear up

Dependence on the Holy Spirit brings victory

Live by the Spirit, and you will not *gratify* the desires of the sinful nature.

—GALATIANS 5:16

live by—habitually walk in dependence on
gratify—fulfill

God will judge the sexually immoral

Marriage should be honored by all, and the marriage bed kept pure, for God will judge the adulterer and all the sexually immoral.

—HEBREWS 13:4

The Lord knows how to rescue godly men

The Lord *knows how* to *rescue* godly men from trials.

—2 PETER 2:9

knows how—recognizes how, realizes how
rescue—deliver

Sickness

The prayer of faith will make a sick person well

Is any one of you *sick*? He should call the elders of the church to pray over him and *anoint* him with oil in the name of the Lord. And the prayer offered in faith will make the sick person *well*; the Lord will raise him up.

—JAMES 5:14-15

sick—ill, weak, ailing
anoint—pour out on
well—healed, delivered, rescued

Though outwardly wasting away, we are inwardly renewed

We do not *lose heart*. Though outwardly we are *wasting away*, yet inwardly we are *being renewed* day by day.

—2 CORINTHIANS 4:16

lose heart—give up, become discouraged, become wearied
wasting away—progressively decaying
being renewed—continually renewed

Permanent resurrection bodies await us

We know that if the earthly tent we live in is *destroyed*, we have a building from God, an eternal house in heaven, not built by human hands.

—2 CORINTHIANS 5:1

destroyed—thrown down, dissolved, abolished

> From the very commencement of my Christian life I was led to feel that the promises of the Bible are very real, and that prayer is in sober fact transacting business with God, whether on one's own behalf or on behalf of those for whom one seeks His blessing.
>
> *Hudson Taylor*

Sin

We are forgiven of our sins

In him we have *redemption* through his blood, the *forgiveness* of sins, in accordance with the riches of God's *grace.*

—EPHESIANS 1:7 (see also COLOSSIANS 2:13-14; MATTHEW 26:28)

redemption—ransom, release from sin
forgiveness—pardon, cancellation of all debt
grace—unmerited favor, kindness

God blots out our transgressions

I, even I, am he who *blots out* your transgressions, for my own sake, and remembers your sins no more.

—ISAIAH 43:25

blots out—exterminates, wipes out, washes off

God cleanses the stain of sin from your soul

"Come now, let us reason together," says the LORD. "Though your *sins* are like scarlet, they shall be as *white* as snow; though they are red as crimson, they shall be like wool."

—ISAIAH 1:18

sins—actions contrary to the law of God
white—whitened, spotless, purified

If we do sin, Jesus is our advocate

I write this to you so that you will not *sin.* But if anybody does sin, we have *one who speaks* to the Father in our defense—Jesus Christ, the Righteous One. He is the atoning sacrifice for our sins, and not only for ours but also for the sins of the whole world.

—1 JOHN 2:1-2

sin—do wrong, go against God's law
one who speaks—an advocate, an intercessor, a defense attorney

God cleanses us of sins when we confess to Him

If we *confess* our sins, he is faithful and just and will *forgive* us our sins and purify us from all unrighteousness.

—1 JOHN 1:9

confess—admit, agree, acknowledge
forgive—pardon, remit, cancel

Slander

Those persecuted for righteousness sake are blessed

Blessed are those who are *persecuted* because of righteousness, for theirs is the kingdom of heaven.

—MATTHEW 5:10

blessed—happy, joyful, favored by God
persecuted—harassed, oppressed

Those persecuted for following Jesus are blessed

Blessed are you when people *insult* you, *persecute* you and falsely say all kinds of evil against you because of me. Rejoice and be glad, because great is your reward in heaven.

—MATTHEW 5:11-12

blessed—happy, joyful, favored by God
insult—denounce, rebuke
persecute—harass, oppress

Spiritual Recovery

God gives strength to the weary

He gives *strength* to the weary and *increases* the power of the weak.

—ISAIAH 40:29

strength—vigor, ability, power
increases—multiplies, enlarges

> The doctrines, the promises,
> the messages of love are as fresh
> today as when first spoken.
>
> *Dwight L. Moody*

Christ gives us rest

Come to me, all you who are *weary* and *burdened*, and I will give you *rest*.

—MATTHEW 11:28

weary—tired, labored
burdened—weighted down
rest—refreshment, relief

The Lord renews our strength

Even youths grow tired and weary, and young men stumble and fall; but those who hope in the LORD will *renew* their strength. They will soar on wings like eagles; they will run and not grow weary, they will walk and not be faint.

—ISAIAH 40:30-31

renew—replace, refresh

We are inwardly renewed daily

We do not *lose heart*. Though outwardly we are *wasting away*, yet inwardly we are *being renewed* day by day. For our light and momentary *troubles* are achieving for us an eternal glory that far outweighs them all.

So we *fix our eyes* not on what is seen, but on what is unseen. For what is seen is temporary, but what is unseen is eternal.

—2 CORINTHIANS 4:16-18

lose heart—give up, become discouraged, become wearied

wasting away—progressively decaying

being renewed—continuously renewed

troubles—distresses, tribulations

fix our eyes—look to, take notice of

Stability

God stabilizes the lives of those who delight in Him

If the LORD *delights in* a man's way, he makes his steps *firm*; though he stumble, he will not fall, for the LORD *upholds* him with his hand.

—PSALM 37:23-24

delights in—is pleased with

firm—steadfast, established, secure

upholds—sustains, braces

The one who loves does not stumble

Whoever *loves* his brother *lives* in the light, and there is nothing in him to make him stumble.

—1 JOHN 2:10

loves—actively loves

lives—abides, dwells, remains

Strength

Christ gives us strength for all things

I can do *everything* through him who gives me *strength*.

—PHILIPPIANS 4:13

everything—all things, anything

strength—inner empowerment

God's power is made perfect in weakness

My grace is sufficient for you, for my power is *made perfect* in weakness.
—2 CORINTHIANS 12:9

made perfect—fulfilled, completed

The Lord renews our strength

Those who *hope in* the LORD will *renew* their strength. They will *soar* on wings like eagles; they will run and not grow weary, they will walk and not be faint.
—ISAIAH 40:31

hope in—wait for, look for
renew—replace, refresh
soar—be lifted up, exalted

God is our strength

God is our *refuge* and *strength*, an ever-present *help* in trouble.
—PSALM 46:1

refuge—shelter
strength—stronghold, fortification
help—support, ally

God will strengthen us

My hand will *sustain* him; surely my arm will strengthen him.
—PSALM 89:21

sustain—establish, uphold

God gives strength to the weary

He gives *strength* to the weary and *increases* the power of the weak.
—ISAIAH 40:29 (see also PSALM 29:11; 2 THESSALONIANS 3:3)

strength—vigor, ability, power
increases—multiplies, enlarges

Stress

Turning anxieties over to God yields perfect peace

Do not be *anxious* about anything, but in everything, by prayer and *petition*, with thanksgiving, present your requests to God. And the *peace* of God, which *transcends* all understanding, will *guard* your hearts and your minds in Christ Jesus.

—PHILIPPIANS 4:6-7

anxious—worried, concerned, fretful
petition—definite requests
peace—tranquility, serenity
transcends—surpasses, exceeds
guard—shield

God is with you

Do not fear, for I am with you; do not be dismayed, for I am your God. I will *strengthen* you and help you; I will *uphold* you with my righteous right hand.

—ISAIAH 41:10

strengthen—support, establish, harden against difficulties
uphold—take hold of, grasp firmly

You can cast your anxieties on God

Cast all your *anxiety* on him because he cares for you.

—1 PETER 5:7

cast—throw
anxiety—concern, worry

Christ gives us peace

Peace I leave with you; my *peace* I give you. I do not give to you as the world gives. Do not let your hearts be *troubled* and do not be *afraid.*

—JOHN 14:27

peace—tranquility, serenity
troubled—disturbed, terrified, thrown into confusion
afraid—timid, cowardly

Success

The one who delights in God's Word succeeds

Blessed is the man who does not walk in the counsel of the wicked or stand in the way of sinners or sit in the seat of mockers. But his *delight* is in the law of the LORD, and on his law he meditates day and night. He is like a tree planted by streams of water, which yields its fruit in season and whose leaf does not wither. Whatever he does *prospers.*

—PSALM 1:1-3

blessed—happy, joyful, favored by God
delight—pleasure, desire
prospers—succeeds, prevails

The one who meditates on God's Word succeeds

Do not let this Book of the Law *depart* from your mouth; *meditate* on it day and night, so that you may be careful to do everything written in it. Then you will be *prosperous* and successful.

—JOSHUA 1:8

depart—leave, be removed
meditate—mutter silently to oneself
prosperous—successful, prevailing

Suffering

God delivers us from troubles

A righteous man may have many troubles, but the LORD delivers him from them all.

—PSALM 34:19

Christ our comfort overflows in our lives

Just as the sufferings of Christ flow over into our lives, so also through Christ our *comfort overflows.*

—2 CORINTHIANS 1:5

comfort—consolation, encouragement
overflows—is superabundant, with more than enough

God brings restoration

The God of all *grace*, who called you to his eternal glory in Christ, after you have suffered a little while, will himself *restore* you and make you strong, firm and steadfast.

—1 PETER 5:10

grace—unmerited favor
restore—mend, make complete

Every promise is built upon four pillars: God's justice and holiness, which will not suffer him to deceive; his grace or goodness, which will not suffer him to forget; his truth, which will not suffer him to change; his power, which makes him able to accomplish.

Salter

We participate in the sufferings of Christ

Do not be *surprised* at the painful trial you are suffering, as though something strange were happening to you. But rejoice that you *participate* in the sufferings of Christ, so that you may be *overjoyed* when his glory is revealed.

—1 PETER 4:12-13 (see also ROMANS 8:16-17)

surprised—astonished
participate—share in
overjoyed—filled with delight

God uses hardship to discipline us

The Lord *disciplines* those he loves, and he *punishes* everyone he accepts as a *son. Endure* hardship as discipline; God is treating you as sons.

—HEBREWS 12:6-7

disciplines—instructs, educates, trains
punishes—scourges, chastises
son—endeared child
endure—patiently endure, persevere

Our present sufferings pale in comparison to our future glory

I consider that our present *sufferings* are not worth comparing with the glory that will be revealed in us.

—ROMANS 8:18

sufferings—misfortunes

Sufficiency of Jesus

God will meet all our needs in Jesus

My God will *meet* all your needs according to his glorious riches in Christ Jesus.

—PHILIPPIANS 4:19

meet—liberally fulfill, complete

We can do all things through Christ who gives us strength

I can do *everything* through him who gives me *strength*.

—PHILIPPIANS 4:13

everything—all things, anything
strength—inner empowerment

We have spiritual blessings in Christ

Praise be to the God and Father of our Lord Jesus Christ, who has *blessed* us in the heavenly realms with every spiritual blessing in Christ.

—EPHESIANS 1:3

blessed—imparted benefits to

Jesus sets us free

If the Son *sets you free*, you will be free *indeed*.

—JOHN 8:36

sets you free—liberates you, frees you from bondage
indeed—surely, certainly, truly, really

Jesus' strength is made perfect in human weakness

My grace is sufficient for you, for my power is *made perfect* in weakness.

—2 CORINTHIANS 12:9

made perfect—fulfilled, completed

Those who believe in Jesus are spiritually satisfied

Jesus declared, "I am the bread of life. He who comes to me will *never* go hungry, and he who *believes in* me will never be thirsty."

—JOHN 6:35

never—absolutely never
believes in—trusts in, puts faith in, relies on

Supplication

Ask and it will be given to you

Ask and it will be given to you; *seek* and you will find; *knock* and the door will be opened to you. For everyone who asks receives; he who seeks finds; and to him who knocks, the door will be opened.

—MATTHEW 7:7-8 (see also LUKE 11:9-11)

ask—keep on asking
seek—keep on seeking
knock—keep on knocking

God answers prayer when we believe

If you *believe*, you will receive whatever you ask for in prayer.

—MATTHEW 21:22

believe—trust, have faith

God answers prayer when we abide in Christ

If you *remain* in me and my words *remain* in you, ask whatever you wish, and it will be given you.

—JOHN 15:7

remain—abide, dwell, live

God answers prayer when two or more agree

If two of you on earth *agree* about *anything* you ask for, it will be done for you by my Father in heaven. For where two or three come together in my name, there am I with them.

—MATTHEW 18:19-20

agree—are in harmony
anything—anything and everything

God answers prayer when we pray in Jesus' name

Until now you have not asked for anything in my name. Ask and you will receive, and your *joy* will be *complete.*

—JOHN 16:24 (see also JOHN 14:13-14)

joy—happiness, rejoicing, gladness
complete—fulfilled

T

Temptation

God can deliver you from any temptation

No *temptation* has *seized* you except what is common to man. And God is faithful; he will not let you be tempted beyond what you can *bear.* But when you are tempted, he will also provide a *way out* so that you can *stand up* under it.

—1 CORINTHIANS 10:13

temptation—trial, enticement to sin
seized—laid hold of, overtaken
bear—endure, resist
way out—means of escape
stand up—endure, bear up

Dependence on the Spirit brings victory

Live by the Spirit, and you will not *gratify* the desires of the sinful nature.

—GALATIANS 5:16

live by—habitually walk in dependence on
gratify—fulfill

Jesus helps us in our temptations

Because he himself suffered when he was tempted, he is able to *help* those who are being tempted.

—HEBREWS 2:18

help—come to the aid of, assist, relieve

The Lord knows how to rescue godly men

The Lord *knows* how to *rescue* godly men from trials.

—2 PETER 2:9

knows—recognizes how, realizes how
rescue—deliver

> There is not a despondent soul but God has a promise just to suit him.
>
> *Dwight L. Moody*

Jesus is sympathetic with our weaknesses and can help us

We do not have a high priest who is unable to *sympathize* with our *weaknesses,* but we have one who has been tempted in every way, just as we are—yet was without sin. Let us then approach the throne of grace with *confidence,* so that we may receive mercy and find grace to help us in our time of need.

—HEBREWS 4:15-16

sympathize—understand, have a shared feeling
weaknesses—infirmities
confidence—boldness, frankness, openness

We are conquerors through Jesus

In all these things we are more than conquerors through him who loved us.

—ROMANS 8:37

Tongue

Every tongue will confess Jesus as Lord

God exalted him to the highest place and gave him the name that is above every name, that at the name of Jesus every knee should bow, in heaven and on earth and under the earth, and every tongue *confess* that Jesus Christ is Lord, to the glory of God the Father.

—PHILIPPIANS 2:9-11

confess—openly confess, admit, consent

Transformation

We are being molded in Christ's image

We, who with unveiled faces all reflect the Lord's glory, are being *transformed* into his *likeness* with ever-increasing glory, which comes from the Lord, who is the Spirit.

—2 CORINTHIANS 3:18

transformed—changed in form, transfigured
likeness—image, portrait

We are transformed by the renewing of our minds

Do not *conform* any longer to the pattern of this world, but be *transformed* by the renewing of your mind. Then you will be able to test and approve what God's will is—his good, pleasing and perfect will.

—ROMANS 12:2

conform—pattern after, fashion after, mold after
transformed—changed in form, molded

God continues to do His work in us

He who began a good *work* in you will carry it on to *completion* until the day of Christ Jesus.

—PHILIPPIANS 1:6

work—activity, task, deed, job
completion—perfection, the finish

Jesus will transform our lowly bodies to be glorious bodies

Our citizenship is in heaven. And we eagerly await a Savior from there, the Lord Jesus Christ, who, by the *power* that enables him to bring everything under his *control*, will *transform* our lowly bodies so that they will be like his glorious body.

—PHILIPPIANS 3:20-21

power—energy
control—subjection, subordination
transform—change the form of, fashion anew

Trials

The Lord knows how to rescue godly men from trials

The Lord *knows* how to *rescue* godly men from trials.

—2 PETER 2:9

knows—recognizes how, realizes how
rescue—deliver

The Lord delivers us from troubles

The righteous cry out, and the LORD hears them; he *delivers* them from all their *troubles*.

—PSALM 34:17

delivers—rescues, saves
troubles—anguishes, calamities, distresses

The Lord will sustain us in our troubles

Cast your *cares* on the LORD and he will *sustain* you; he will never let the righteous fall.

—PSALM 55:22

cast—throw, hurl
cares—burdens
sustain—uphold, support, bear up

Persevere, and you'll receive the crown of life

Blessed is the man who *perseveres* under trial, because when he has stood the test, he will receive the crown of life that God has promised to those who love him.

—JAMES 1:12

perseveres—stands firm, endures

Christ gives us rest

Come to me, all you who are *weary* and *burdened*, and I will give you *rest*.

—MATTHEW 11:28

weary—tired, labored
burdened—weighted down
rest—refreshment, relief

God answers prayer; sometimes,
when hearts are weak,
He gives the very gifts believers seek.
But often faith must learn a deeper rest,
And trust God's silence,
when He does not speak;
For He whose name is Love
will send the best.
Stars may burn out nor
mountain walls endure,
But God is true;
His promises are sure
To those who seek.

M. G. Plantz

T

Trouble

The Lord is a refuge in times of trouble

The LORD is good, a *refuge* in times of *trouble.* He cares for those who trust in him.

—NAHUM 1:7 (see also PSALM 9:9)

refuge—stronghold, place of protection
trouble—distress, calamity

The Lord delivers the righteous from their troubles

The righteous cry out, and the LORD hears them; he *delivers* them from all their *troubles.* The LORD is close to the brokenhearted and saves those who are crushed in spirit.

—PSALM 34:17-18

delivers—spares, saves, rescues
troubles—calamities, anguishes, distresses

God comforts us in all our troubles

Praise be to the God and Father of our Lord Jesus Christ, the Father of *compassion* and the God of all *comfort,* who comforts us in all our *troubles,* so that we can comfort those in any trouble with the comfort we ourselves have received from God.

—2 CORINTHIANS 1:3-4

compassion—mercy, pity
comfort—consolation, encouragement
troubles—distresses, tribulations

If we call upon God, He will deliver us from our troubles

Call upon me in the day of trouble; I will *deliver* you, and you will honor me.

—PSALM 50:15

call upon—summon
deliver—rescue

Even in our troubles, God is working for our good

We know that in all things God works for the *good* of those who *love* him, who have been called according to his purpose.

—ROMANS 8:28

good—positive good, moral good
love—actively love

Christ has overcome the world, and in Him we have peace

I have told you these things, so that in me you may have *peace.* In this world you will have *trouble.* But take heart! I have *overcome* the world.

—JOHN 16:33

peace—tranquility, a sense of welfare, with no fears
trouble—distress, tribulation, oppression
overcome—conquered, triumphed, overpowered

Our momentary troubles are achieving great glory for us

Our light and momentary *troubles* are achieving for us an eternal glory that far outweighs them all. So we *fix our eyes* not on what is seen, but on what is unseen. For what is seen is temporary, but what is unseen is eternal.

—2 CORINTHIANS 4:17-18

troubles—distresses, tribulations
fix our eyes—look to, take notice of

Trust

God cares for those who trust in Him

The LORD is good, a *refuge* in times of *trouble.* He cares for those who trust in him.

—NAHUM 1:7

refuge—stronghold, place of protection
trouble—distress, calamity

The man who trusts the Lord is blessed

Blessed is the man who *trusts in* the LORD, whose *confidence* is in him.

—JEREMIAH 17:7

trusts in—relies on, puts confidence in
confidence—security, firm trust

Blessed is the man who makes the LORD his *trust*, who does not look to the proud, to those who turn aside to false gods.

—PSALM 40:4

blessed—happy, joyful, favored by God
trust—security, confidence

The Lord's love surrounds the one who trusts in Him

Many are the *woes* of the wicked, but the LORD's *unfailing love surrounds* the man who trusts in him.

—PSALM 32:10

woes—griefs, sorrows, sufferings
unfailing love—loyal love, unfailing devotion
surrounds—encircles, engulfs

Peace accompanies the one who trusts in God

You will *keep* in *perfect peace* him whose mind is steadfast, because he trusts in you. Trust in the LORD forever, for the LORD, the LORD, is the Rock eternal.

—ISAIAH 26:3-4

keep—guard
perfect—complete and constant
peace—well-being, wholeness, tranquility

Truth

The Spirit of truth guides us into all truth

When he, the Spirit of truth, comes, he will *guide* you into all truth.
—JOHN 16:13

guide—lead, explain, instruct

God's Word provides us truth

The law of the LORD is *perfect*, *reviving* the soul. The statutes of the LORD are trustworthy, making wise the simple. The precepts of the LORD are right, giving *joy* to the heart. The commands of the LORD are radiant, giving light to the eyes. The *fear* of the LORD is pure, enduring forever. The ordinances of the LORD are sure and altogether righteous.
—PSALM 19:7-9

perfect—blameless, without defect
reviving—recovering, restoring
joy—rejoicing, delight
fear—worshipful fear, show reverence to

The truth sets us free

You will *know* the truth, and the truth will *set you free*.
—JOHN 8:32

know—recognize, understand
set you free—liberate you, free you from bondage

The Lord is near to those who call on Him in truth

The LORD is near to all who call on him, to all who call on him in *truth*.
—PSALM 145:18

truth—sincerity

U-V

Victory

We are conquerors in Christ

In all these things we are more than conquerors through him who *loved* us.

—ROMANS 8:37

loved—actively loved

We have peace in Jesus the Conqueror

I have told you these things, so that in me you may have *peace*. In this world you will have *trouble*. But take heart! I have *overcome* the world.

—JOHN 16:33

peace—tranquility, serenity
trouble—distress, tribulation, oppression
overcome—conquered, triumphed, overpowered

With God we will gain the victory

With God we will gain the victory, and he will trample down our enemies.

—PSALM 60:12

Everyone born of God overcomes the world

Everyone born of God *overcomes* the world. This is the victory that has overcome the world, even our faith. Who is it that *overcomes* the world? Only he who believes that Jesus is the Son of God.

—1 JOHN 5:4-5

overcomes—triumphs over, overpowers, conquers

God will crush Satan

The God of *peace* will soon *crush* Satan under your feet.

—Romans 16:20

peace—tranquility, serenity, well-being, welfare
crush—break, dash to pieces, destroy

Death will be swallowed up in victory

When the perishable has been clothed with the imperishable, and the mortal with immortality, then the saying that is written will come true: "Death has been *swallowed up* in victory."

—1 Corinthians 15:54

swallowed up—overwhelmed, drowned

> Our Lord has written the promise of the resurrection, not in books alone, but in every leaf in springtime.
>
> *Martin Luther*

W-X-Y-Z

Waiting on God

The Savior will return and transform us

Our citizenship is in heaven. And we eagerly await a Savior from there, the Lord Jesus Christ, who, by the *power* that enables him to bring everything under his *control*, will *transform* our lowly bodies so that they will be like his glorious body.

—Philippians 3:20-21

power—energy
control—subjection, subordination
transform—change the form of, fashion anew

Blessed are all who wait for God

The LORD *longs* to be *gracious* to you; he rises to show you *compassion.* For the LORD is a God of justice. Blessed are all who wait for him!

—ISAIAH 30:18

longs—lies in wait, hopes for

gracious—charming, kind, merciful, compassionate

compassion—mercy, pity

The Lord is good to those who wait on Him

The LORD is good to those whose hope is in him, to the one who seeks him; it is good to wait quietly for the *salvation* of the LORD.

—LAMENTATIONS 3:25-26

salvation—rescue, victory

Christ will bring final salvation to those who wait for Him

Christ was sacrificed once to take away the *sins* of many people; and he will appear a second time, not to bear sin, but to bring *salvation* to those who are waiting for him.

—HEBREWS 9:28

sins—wrongdoings, acts contrary to God's law

salvation—ultimate rescue, ultimate deliverance

Weakness

God increases the power of the weak

He gives *strength* to the weary and *increases* the power of the weak.

—ISAIAH 40:29

strength—vigor, ability, power

increases—multiplies, enlarges

God's power is made perfect in weakness

My grace is sufficient for you, for my power is *made perfect* in weakness.

—2 CORINTHIANS 12:9

made perfect—fulfilled, completed

Christ sympathizes with our weaknesses

We do not have a high priest who is unable to *sympathize* with our *weaknesses*, but we have one who has been tempted in every way, just as we are—yet was without sin.

—HEBREWS 4:15

sympathize—understand, have a shared feeling

weaknesses—infirmities

The Spirit helps us in our weakness

The Spirit himself *intercedes* for us with groans that words cannot express.

—ROMANS 8:26

intercedes—pleads, prays

God blesses those who help the weak

Blessed is he who has regard for the *weak*; the LORD *delivers* him in times of trouble. The LORD will *protect* him and preserve his life.

—PSALM 41:1-2

blessed—happy, joyful, favored by God

weak—poor, needy, scrawny

delivers—saves, rescues

protect—guard, watch over

Will of God

God will guide us

I will *instruct* you and *teach* you in the way you should go; I will *counsel* you and watch over you.

—PSALM 32:8

instruct—give understanding, insight, wisdom
teach—give guidance to
counsel—advise, give direction to

God gives us wisdom if we ask in faith

If any of you *lacks* wisdom, he should ask God, who gives *generously* to all without finding fault, and it will be given to him.

—JAMES 1:5

lacks—is deficient in
generously—without reserve, liberally, ungrudgingly

Minds transformed by God's Word can discern His will

Do not *conform* any longer to the pattern of this world, but be *transformed* by the renewing of your mind. Then you will be able to test and approve what God's will is—his good, pleasing and perfect will.

—ROMANS 12:2

conform—pattern after, fashion after, mold after
transformed—changed in form, molded

The Lord makes our steps firm

If the LORD *delights in* a man's way, he makes his steps *firm.*

—PSALM 37:23

delights in—is pleased with, has pleasure in
firm—established, steadfast, prepared

God is our guide to the very end of our lives

This God is our God for ever and ever; he will be our guide even to the *end.*

—PSALM 48:14

end—death

Wisdom

God gives wisdom to those who ask in faith

If any of you *lacks* wisdom, he should ask God, who gives *generously* to all without finding fault, and it will be given to him.

—JAMES 1:5

lacks—is deficient in

generously—without reserve, liberally, ungrudgingly

God is a rich store of wisdom

He will be the *sure* foundation for your times, a rich store of salvation and *wisdom* and *knowledge;* the *fear* of the LORD is the key to this treasure.

—ISAIAH 33:6

sure—faithful, steady, trustworthy

wisdom—skill for living

knowledge—understanding, learning

fear—worshipful fear, show reverence to

God's Word makes us wise

The law of the LORD is *perfect, reviving* the soul. The statutes of the LORD are trustworthy, making wise the simple. The precepts of the LORD are right, giving *joy* to the heart. The commands of the LORD are radiant, giving light to the eyes.

—PSALM 19:7-8

perfect—blameless, without defect

reviving—recovering, restoring

joy—rejoicing, delight

Word of God

Scripture is inspired and thoroughly equips us

All Scripture is *God-breathed* and is *useful* for teaching, rebuking, correcting and training in righteousness, so that the man of God may be *thoroughly equipped* for every good work.

—2 TIMOTHY 3:16-17

God-breathed—inspired
useful—valuable, profitable
thoroughly equipped—capable of meeting all demands, proficient

Hearing God's Word increases our faith

Faith comes from hearing the message, and the message is heard through the word of Christ.

—ROMANS 10:17

faith—belief, trust

Meditating on God's Word leads to prosperity

Do not let this Book of the Law *depart* from your mouth; *meditate* on it day and night, so that you may be careful to do everything written in it. Then you will be prosperous and successful.

—JOSHUA 1:8

depart—leave, be removed
meditate—mutter silently to yourself

> [George Muller] found God's promises in the Bible and experienced the truth of them in his everyday life. He learned to believe what he read and to act accordingly. He mined religious truth, not from books of human fabrication, but from God through divine inspiration, and what he read he lived.
>
> *Basil Miller*

Being doers of the Word brings blessing

Do not merely listen to the word, and so *deceive* yourselves. *Do* what it says. Anyone who listens to the word but does not do what it says is like a man who looks at his face in a mirror and, after looking at himself, goes away and immediately forgets what he looks like. But the man who looks intently into the perfect law that gives freedom, and continues to do this, not forgetting what he has heard, but doing it—he will be *blessed* in what he does.

—JAMES 1:22-25

deceive—delude
do—obey, keep
blessed—happy, fortunate, favored by God

God's Word stands forever

The grass withers and the flowers fall, but the word of our God *stands* forever.

—ISAIAH 40:8 (see also 1 PETER 1:23-25)

stands—is established, is confirmed

Work

Our work will be rewarded

Whatever you do, work at it with all your heart, as working for the Lord, not for men, since you know that you will receive an inheritance from the Lord as a reward. It is the Lord Christ you are *serving.*

—COLOSSIANS 3:23-24

serving—serving as a slave

Your labor is not in vain

Let nothing move you. Always give yourselves *fully* to the work of the Lord, because you know that your labor in the Lord is not *in vain.*

—1 CORINTHIANS 15:58

fully—in an abundant way, in an overflowing way
in vain—empty, empty-handed, useless, ineffective

God gives you what you need to do every good work

God is able to make all *grace abound* to you, so that in all things at all times, having all that you need, you will *abound* in every good work.

—2 CORINTHIANS 9:8

grace—unmerited favor, kindness
abound—overflow

Christ gives rest to the overworked

Come to me, all you who are *weary* and *burdened,* and I will give you *rest.*

—MATTHEW 11:28

weary—tired, labored
burdened—weighted down
rest—refreshment, relief

World

You need not be conformed to this world

Do not *conform* any longer to the pattern of this world, but be *transformed* by the renewing of your mind. Then you will be able to test and approve what God's will is—his good, pleasing and perfect will.

—Romans 12:2

conform—pattern after, fashion after, mold after
transformed—changed in form, molded

Those who do the will of God live forever

Do not love the *world* or anything in the world. If anyone loves the world, the love of the Father is not in him. For everything in the world—the cravings of sinful man, the lust of his eyes and the boasting of what he has and does—comes not from the Father but from the world. The world and its *desires* pass away, but the man who does the will of God lives forever.

—1 John 2:15-17

world—anti-God system over which Satan rules
desires—longings, cravings, lusts

Heavenly treasures cannot be lost

Do not *store up* for yourselves treasures on earth, where moth and rust *destroy*, and where thieves break in and steal. But *store up* for yourselves treasures in heaven, where moth and rust do not *destroy*, and where thieves do not break in and steal. For where your treasure is, there your heart will be also.

—Matthew 6:19-21

store up—gather, reserve
destroy—cause to perish, vanish, disappear

Jesus is the light of the world

I have come into the world as a light, so that no one who *believes in* me should stay in darkness.

—JOHN 12:46

believes in—trusts in, puts faith in, relies on

Christ has overcome the world, and in Him we have peace

I have told you these things, so that in me you may have *peace.* In this world you will have *trouble.* But take heart! I have *overcome* the world.

—JOHN 16:33

peace—tranquility, serenity

trouble—distress, tribulation, oppression

overcome—conquered, triumphed, overpowered

Worry

Turning anxieties over to God yields perfect peace

Do not be *anxious* about anything, but in everything, by prayer and *petition,* with thanksgiving, present your requests to God. And the *peace* of God, which *transcends* all understanding, will *guard* your hearts and your minds in Christ Jesus.

—PHILIPPIANS 4:6-7

anxious—worried, concerned, fretful

petition—definite requests

peace—tranquility, serenity

transcends—surpasses, exceeds

guard—shield

The Lord sustains us in our troubles

Cast your *cares* on the LORD and he will *sustain* you; he will never let the righteous fall.

—PSALM 55:22

cast—throw, hurl
cares—burdens
sustain—uphold, support, bear up

God will meet all our needs

My God will *meet* all your needs according to his glorious riches in Christ Jesus.

—PHILIPPIANS 4:19

meet—liberally fulfill, complete

God is our refuge and strength

God is our *refuge* and *strength*, an ever-present *help* in trouble.

—PSALM 46:1

refuge—shelter
strength—stronghold, fortification
help—support, ally

Christ gives us peace

Peace I leave with you; my *peace* I give you. I do not give to you as the world gives. Do not let your hearts be *troubled* and do not be *afraid.*

—JOHN 14:27

peace—tranquility, serenity
troubled—disturbed, terrified, thrown into confusion
afraid—timid, cowardly

The mind focused on God is in perfect peace

You will *keep* in *perfect peace* him whose mind is steadfast, because he trusts in you. Trust in the LORD forever, for the LORD, the LORD, is the Rock eternal.

—ISAIAH 26:3-4

keep—guard
perfect—complete and constant
peace—tranquility, serenity

God's Covenant Promises

A covenant is a promise-agreement between two parties. A covenant is a special kind of foundational promise. Covenants were used among the ancients in the form of treaties or alliances between nations (1 Samuel 11:1), treaties between individual people (Genesis 21:27), friendship pacts (1 Samuel 18:3), and agreements between God and His people.

In the Bible, God made specific covenant promises to a number of people, including Noah (Genesis 9:8-17), Abraham (Genesis 15: 12-21; 17:1-14), the Israelites at Mount Sinai (Exodus 19:5-6), David (2 Samuel 7:13; 23:5), and God's people in the New Covenant (Hebrews 8:6-13). In what follows, I will summarize the more important of these covenants.

1. Abrahamic Covenant. A very famous covenant is God's covenant with Abraham (Genesis 12:1-3; 15:18-21), which was later reaffirmed with Isaac (17:21) and Jacob (35:10-12). In this covenant, God promised to make Abraham's descendants His own special people. More specifically, God promised Abraham: 1) I will make you a great nation; 2) I will bless you; 3) I will make your name great; 4) You will be a blessing; 5) I will bless those who bless you; 6) I will curse those who curse you; and 7) All peoples on earth will be blessed through you.

These covenant promises were unconditional in nature. A *conditional* covenant is a covenant with an "if" attached. This type of covenant demanded that the people meet certain obligations or conditions before God was obligated to fulfill that which was promised. If God's people failed in meeting the conditions, God was not obligated in any way to fulfill the promise.

As opposed to this, an *unconditional* covenant depended on no such conditions for its fulfillment. There were no "ifs" attached. That which was promised was sovereignly given to the recipient of the covenant apart from any merit (or lack thereof) on the part of the recipient. The covenant God made with Abraham was unconditional.

The promises God made to Abraham must have seemed incredible. After all, God promised him that his descendants would be as numerous as the stars in the sky (Genesis 12:1-3; 13:14-17). The promise must have seemed unbelievable to Abraham since his wife was childless (11:30). Yet Abraham did not doubt God; he knew God would faithfully give what He had promised. God even reaffirmed the covenant in Genesis 15, perhaps to emphasize to Abraham that even in his advanced age, the promise would come to pass.

At one point, an impatient Sarah suggested that their heir might be procured through their Egyptian handmaiden, Hagar. Ishmael was thus born to Abraham, through Hagar, when he was 86 years old. But Ishmael was *not* the child of promise. In God's perfect timing, the child of promise was finally born when Abraham and Sarah were very old (Abraham was 100), far beyond normal childbearing age. They named their son Isaac (Genesis 21), and, as promised, an entire nation eventually developed from his line. *Isaac* means "laughter" and is a fitting name because it points to the joy derived from this child of promise.

2. Davidic Covenant. God later made a covenant with David in which He promised that one of his descendants would rule forever (2 Samuel 7:12-13; 22:51). This is another example of an unconditional covenant. It did not depend on David in any way for its fulfillment. David realized this when he received the promise from God, and responded with an attitude of humility and a recognition of God's sovereignty over the affairs of men. This covenant finds its ultimate fulfillment in Jesus Christ, who was born from the line of David (Matthew 1:1).

3. Sinai Covenant. God's covenant with Israel at Mount Sinai, following Israel's sojourn through the wilderness after being delivered from Egypt, constituted the formal basis of the redemptive relationship between God and the Israelites (Exodus 19:3-25). This covenant was couched in terms of ancient Hittite suzerainty treaties made between kings and their subjects. Such treaties would always include a preamble naming the author of the treaty, a historical introduction depicting the relationship between the respective parties, a list of stipulations explaining the responsibilities of each of the parties, a promise of either blessing or judgment invoked depending on faithfulness or unfaithfulness to the treaty, a solemn oath, and a religious ratification of the treaty. In such treaties, the motivation for obedience to the stipulations was the undeserved favor of the king making the treaty. Out of gratitude, the people were to obey the stipulations.

Such parallels between ancient treaties and God's covenant with Israel show that God communicated to His people in ways they were familiar with. Key parallels between such treaties and the Sinai Covenant are that God gave stipulations to the people explaining their responsibilities (the law, Exodus 20:1-17) and gave a promise of blessing for obeying the law and a promise of judgment for disobeying the law (see Exodus 19:5-8; 24:3,7). Sadly, Israel was often disobedient to God's covenant (Exodus 32:1-31; Jeremiah 31:32). In this covenant, blessing was conditioned on obedience.

Old Testament history is replete with illustrations of how unfaithful Israel was to the covenant. The two most significant periods of exile for the Jewish people involved the fall of Israel to the Assyrians in 722 B.C. and the collapse of Judah under Babylonian siege in 597-581 B.C. As God promised, disobedience brought exile to God's own people.

The first chapter of Isaiah takes the form of a lawsuit against Judah. Judah was indicted by the Lord (through Isaiah) because of Judah's "breach of contract" in breaking the Sinai Covenant, which had been given to the nation at the time of the Exodus from Egypt. In this courtroom scene, the Lord called upon heaven and earth to act as witnesses to the accusations leveled against the nation (Isaiah 1:2). The whole universe was to bear witness that God's judgments are just.

The Lord indicted Judah for rebelling against Him. The Hebrew word for "rebel" in Isaiah 1:2 was often used among the ancients in reference to a subordinate state's violation of treaty with a sovereign nation. In Isaiah 1, the word points to Judah's blatant violation of God's covenant. Therefore, Israel went into captivity.

In this case, the Babylonian captivity was God's means of chastening Judah. Of course, God intended this judgment to be corrective. Throughout both the Old and New Testaments, we find that God disciplines His children to purify them. Just as an earthly father disciplines his children, so God the Father disciplines His children to train and educate them (Hebrews 12:1-6).

4. The New Covenant. The New Covenant is an unconditional covenant God made with humankind in which He promised to provide for forgiveness of sin, based entirely on the sacrificial death and resurrection of Jesus Christ (Jeremiah 31:31-34). Under the Old Covenant, worshipers never enjoyed a sense of total forgiveness. Under the New Covenant, however, Christ our High Priest made provision for such forgiveness. When Jesus ate the Passover meal with the disciples in the Upper Room, He spoke of the cup as "the new covenant in my blood" (Luke 22:20; see also 1 Corinthians 11:25). Jesus has done all that is necessary for the forgiveness of sins by His once-and-for-all sacrifice on the cross. This New Covenant is the basis for our relationship with God in the New Testament.

Resources

The following resources were very helpful in deriving insights on Greek and Hebrew words and collecting quotes:

Books

1. *Drapers Book of Quotations for the Christian World* (Grand Rapids, MI: Baker Book House, 1992).
2. William MacDonald, *Believer's Bible Commentary* (Nashville, TN: Thomas Nelson Publishers, 1995).
3. Larry Richards, *Every Promise in the Bible* (Nashville, TN: Thomas Nelson Publishing, 1998).

Software

1. Accordance Bible Software, published by Oaksoft Software
2. HyperCard stack, published by Apple Computer, Inc.
3. Sage Digital Library, published by Sage Software

Web sites

1. <www.cyberhymnal.org>

Books You Can Believe In™
HARVEST HOUSE PUBLISHERS

The Complete Book of Bible Answers
Ron Rhodes

This great resource addresses the difficult Bible questions that arise during Bible studies and witnessing—covering topics that range from the conflicts between science and the Bible to reconciling God's sovereignty with man's free will.

Find It Fast in the Bible
Ron Rhodes

A quick reference that lives up to its name! With more than 400 topics and 8000-plus references, this comprehensive, topical guide provides one-line summaries of each verse. Perfect for research, discussions, and Bible studies.

Find It Quick Handy Bible Encyclopedia
Ron Rhodes

Complete enough to be called an encyclopedia but compact enough to be quick and easy to use, this reference book includes approximately 1500 entries, each containing concise definitions, interesting information, and Scripture references.

Can You Trust the Bible?
Ralph O. Muncaster

Tracing the advancement of writing and materials, this Examine the Evidence book reveals how the Bible was written and accuracy maintained, how historical and archaeological evidence proves translation integrity, and how the canon was developed.

Is the Bible Really a Message from God?
Ralph O. Muncaster

Part of the Examine the Evidence series, this book highlights the biblical proof that God exists and communicates with us. Readers will explore the Bible's inspiration, accuracy, and its impact on day-to-day living.

The Stones Cry Out
Randall Price

Recently uncovered ancient artifacts shed light upon the lives of the patriarchs, the Ark of the Covenant, the fall of Jericho, King David, and more. More than 80 photos demonstrate the incontrovertible facts that support biblical truth.